HOSPITAL SOCIAL WORK IN INDIA

DR. MUKESH KUMAR

ATLANTIC
PUBLISHERS & DISTRIBUTORS (P) LTD

ATLANTIC
PUBLISHERS & DISTRIBUTORS (P) LTD

7/22, Ansari Road, Darya Ganj, New Delhi
Tel.: +91-11-4077 5252, 2327 3880
E-mail: orders@atlanticbooks.com
Web: www.atlanticbooks.com

Published by Atlantic Publishers & Distributors (P) Ltd 2024

Printed & bound in India by Atlantic Print Services

Dedicated to

Social work professionals for their valuable contributions to the field of healthcare.

Preface

Hospital Social Work is an important and well-recognized area of engagement for professional social workers. The recommendations of the Health Survey and Development Committee, popularly known as the Bhore Committee (1946), paved the way for the training and placement of professional social workers in hospital settings. Following the recommendations of the committee, the Tata Institute of Social Sciences, Mumbai started providing specialized training in medical and psychiatric social work in 1948 and since then, many institutions have been offering specialization in this field. Further, the guidelines as laid down by the Medical Council of India (1999) and Indian Public Health Standards for District Hospitals (2012) also recommended the appointment of medical and psychiatric social workers in hospitals and medical colleges. Trained social workers are also appointed in the implementation of various health programmes run by the government. However, progress in the area of hospital social work has been very slow and professional social workers have been struggling with several issues pertaining to their appointments in medical settings.

The present book attempts to explore, understand and analyze the domain of hospital social work in the Indian context through scientific study. It covers certain important aspects of social work practice in health settings that require significant attention, including the critical exploration of the role of hospital social workers. On the basis of the results of the study, the book provides specific recommendations for the responsibilities of hospital social workers, hospitals, schools of social work, professional organizations and government. The suggestions given in this study could be of effective use in revisiting and consolidating social work practice in medical settings.

Many people have been instrumental in bringing about this book in its current format and I am deeply indebted to them for their kind cooperation and encouragement. At the outset, I express my heartfelt gratitude to Prof. Gracious Thomas, School of Social Work, Indira Gandhi National Open University (IGNOU), for providing his persistent guidance and supervision in completing this work. He is a true visionary who has contributed immensely to the discipline of social work and has been an authority in this field for many years. It is with his plenteous support and focused direction that the work has been accomplished in this conformation. I am extremely thankful to other faculty members at the School of Social Work, IGNOU, for providing their valuable guidance and relevant inputs in the process of completing the study.

I am grateful to the hospital authorities in Delhi for permitting me to collect the data. I offer heartfelt gratitude to the professional social workers whom I interviewed, for giving their precious time and providing the relevant information with great enthusiasm. The interactions held with them during the data collection were, indeed, the most memorable moments in the process.

I am indebted to all my fellow companions with whom I stayed connected throughout the study.

Finally, I owe a special word of thanks to Atlantic Publishers and Distributors (P) Ltd. for their keen interest and support in the publication of this book.

Dr. Mukesh Kumar

Contents

1
Introduction

Since inception, hospitals have performed multiple functions ranging from serving as hospices for the pilgrims to providing organized medical facilities that offer patient care, bio-social research and training of required manpower in the field of healthcare. Modern hospitals are envisaged as complex organizations that are licensed by the appropriate authority and mobilize the skills and efforts of multiple medical, para-medical and non-medical staff to render highly personalized services to patients. Broadly, hospitals are dealing with the functions of receiving, classifying, diagnosing, treating, maintaining and discharging. Describing the activities of hospitals, Mathew (1979) has classified those into therapeutic functions and administrative functions. Therapeutic functions involve interaction with the patients and dealing with their clinical and social management. These functions are performed by three types of functionaries, namely (a) professionals, (b) technicians, (c) non-professionals. Administrative Maintenance covers executive functions, organization and maintenance-oriented functions, training and research. These functions are performed by the superintendent, manager, accountant, building maintenance staff, laundry staff and librarian.

Healthcare personnel can be classified into numerous categories. Greenfield (1969) divides health professionals into four separate groups. First, the autonomous professionals include physicians, surgeons, dentists and others. Second, the allied health professionals include nurses, psychologists, pharmacists, medical social workers and others. Third, the allied health technicians include X-ray technicians, nurses with an associate or diploma degree, medical technicians and medical and technical assistance. Fourth, the allied health assistants include licensed practical nurses, nurses' aides and other categories of aid professionals. It was only recently that the hospital authorities gained awareness to run hospitals in an efficient and organized way, apart from maintaining their image as a service organization, where hospital social workers emerged in response to the specific needs of patients.

Social Work: A Vital Hospital Function

The presence of social workers in the hospital is important in the interest of patients, doctors and the community.

Patients visit hospitals to seek clarification about their medical conditions and treatment advice. The doctor applies the knowledge and skill to diagnose the illness and suggests the required therapeutic modality. The scientific methods of medicine soon establish anemia, diabetes, heart disease, peptic ulcer or possibly a functional disorder. When the diagnosis is known, the doctor promptly looks to implement the treatment plan to ensure the best possible result for the patient. In the meantime, the patient who came seeking relief from pain or because of undue fatigue or failing capacities has endured several clinical examinations, investigations and procedures that he often does not understand or finds sometimes unpleasant and threatening. In the medical assessment, they may experience much of the complexity of the modern hospital. They go from one place to another with mysterious slips of reference. They learn many things that were not expected when he came. Recommendations are made beyond his ability to carry out. They are asked to return for review, to be admitted for operation, to live with a permanent handicap, or to accept the idea of chronic disease and adjust to it. The patient may build anxieties, fears and confusion (McMahon, 1958). Thus, trained social workers could be a link for patients in navigating hospital procedures and protocols.

It is also essential to learn that the patient understands the illness and medical treatment prescribed by the physician. The anxieties, fears, tensions, misunderstandings and areas of misinterpretation are required to be discovered and sorted to ensure the effective participation of the patient in the process of treatment. The presence of social workers is important in helping patients and their families to manage social and emotional aspects of illness and disease. Bartlett (1961) has rightly said that body illness is a reality problem with a large social and emotional component, which is not merely the result of illness but needs treatment throughout the illness. Illness generates emotional stress in the patient and other significant ones. More severely, it brings isolation, helplessness, discomfort, dependency, uncertainty and fear for the sick person. She further emphasized that social and emotional stressors shall not be regarded as results only; rather, these are primarily the components of illness throughout its course of treatment. To help individuals cope with these stresses, one requires skills other than those of the medical profession. There has been a gradual realization that consideration of the patient as a person in a complex environment and as an organism subjected to many stresses and strains calls for the collaborative teamwork of persons of multiple disciplines. Social workers as a group were recognized as one of the professionals who have a definite role to play.

Healthcare facilities in the country have evolved tremendously in the last few decades. The advancement in the field of medical technology has made it possible to cure diseases that were once considered incurable. However, the cost of their treatment is so high that their affordability remains out of reach for many patients. From drugs and surgeries to other medical procedures, nothing costs less than a few lakh rupees. Social workers, being experts in making socio-economic assessments and mobilizing resources available within and outside the client systems, can be very handy in this situation.

Medical social workers bridge the gap in the relationship between doctors and patients. A certain degree of self-fulfillment in the practice of medicine passed away with the disappearance of the family doctor. Its place has been taken by scientific achievements through striving for greater exactness and technical perfection. This requires the application of wider knowledge and impersonal and objective thinking, which leaves practically no room for personal human interaction. Though scientific knowledge and technological advancement have resulted in the precision of patient care, there has been an erosion of the doctor-patient relationship, and care has become more fragmented (Anand, 2019). This fragmented approach to care cannot accelerate the process of helping sick individuals reach an optimal level of health, as it fails to deal with the social component of illness. The undesirable but unavoidable increases in the clinic caseload of the individual physician in the hospital and the unavoidable decrease in the frequency with which the physician can maintain a close personal relation with patients have contributed to the progress of this specialized social service activity in hospital settings.

Hospitals and medical colleges required expertise of social workers in investigating into the psychological and social components of health and illness-related behaviors. Merged or affiliated institutions with a major university teaching hospital are becoming commonplace and are seen as offering many advantages to patients, physicians and other healthcare professionals in joining educational, research, as well as capital equipment resources (Sheps, 1973). The academic health center, under the aegis of the university, has a profound influence on the operational services of its teaching hospitals. They also have been the beneficiaries of a great deal of medical research and education monies. Although the academic medical center's significant concentration is on quality of care, this concentration is predominantly biomedical. Factors such as access, effectiveness, economy and equity of services arise more out of social and community pressure to examine them than as fundamentals to the delivery of medical services. Individuals suffering from the newly recognized social ailments of substance abuse, child, wife and parent abuse enter the academic medical center's emergency rooms but in the context of the physical disorder. Although such problems are a major public concern, they are not within the purview of the biologically trained physician. The causes relevant to the before and after situations are not usually addressed. Although the medical profession has accepted the responsibility for the care of patients suffering from such problems, it has not been educated to deal with the complex social problems of today. These social problems call for knowledge from the range of social and behavioral sciences and for treatments and programs with both a psychosocial and medical emphasis as mutually inseparable in the care of these sufferers.

Hospitals often receive specialized and vulnerable groups of patients like children, women, older persons, physically disabled, mentally ill, victims of domestic violence, rape victims, homeless, unknown, illiterate, poor, etc. These patients need necessary support so that they are kept safe in hospital surroundings and discharged to appropriate places. Social work is a value-based profession committed to helping the needy and serving the poorest of the poor; hence, its intervention is desirable in such cases.

Advanced practitioners in clinical social work realize the possible challenging impact of economic, social, and cultural factors on the lives of patients and their systems. They also know the stigma and shame attached to disorders, diagnoses and help-seeking behaviors across varying populations. They also appreciate methods for promoting human rights and social and economic justice in local and global contexts. Clinical social workers use knowledge of the impact of oppression, differentiation and historical trauma on client and client systems to guide treatment planning and intervention. They provide support at multiple levels for mental health parity and the depletion of health inequalities for diverse populations (*Educational Policy and Accreditation Standards* (*EPAS*), 2008, Council for Social Work Education).

Theoretical Frameworks in Hospital Social Work

Bio-Psychosocial Model

The bio-psychosocial model, which was born out of the general system theory, ascertains the assumption that a person encompasses a complex interaction of biological, psychological, social, cultural, spiritual and physical experiences that all impact their life (Fort Cowles, 2003). Hence this model helps to understand people in their totality. Specific to the hospital social worker is the bio-psychosocial approach to practice. "Social work's bio-psychosocial approach provides a carefully balanced perspective, which considers the entire person in his or her environment and helps social workers in screening and assessing the needs of an individual from a multidimensional point of view" (Berkman and Volland, 1997, p. 143). The bio-psychosocial approach takes into account three overlapping aspects of the patient's functioning: "bio" refers to the biological and medical aspects of the patient's health and wellbeing; "psycho" refers to the patient's self-worth, self-esteem and emotional resources as they relate to the medical condition; and "social" refers to the social environment that surrounds and influences the patient. It behooves the social worker to assess each of these domains to gain a full understanding of the patient (Rock, 2002). The model also assumes clinicians must assess all these experiences of the person to effectively provide interventions. In the healthcare setting, often the one who seeks medical treatment experiences other bio-psychosocial challenges that are affecting one's physical health status. In a healthcare setting, medical professionals are experts in treating biological and physical ailments. However, with the assumption that a person is comprised of more than biology, other professionals, such as social workers, who are experts in assessing these other aspects impacting a person's life, are necessary and bring additional efficacy when providing medical intervention.

Person-in-Environment Perspective

The person-in-environment is the guiding principle for social workers that emphasis upon assessing people and their behavior in the light of environment in which they live and act. The unifying theoretical perspective is the perception that clients can better be understood and assisted in the context of the circumstances and resources of their social conditions. Social environment refers to the quality and features of an individual's life situation, including interpersonal relations, personal resources, one's status, roles and participation in society (Cowles, 2000, p. 10). This orientation, known as the person-in-environment, was what motivated Dr. Cabot and Ida Cannon to establish social work in their hospital so that the physicians could enhance their healing potential by having a greater understanding of what their patients had to deal with when they left the hospital. Did patients have people in their immediate environment that could care for them? What supports existed, and what needed to be enhanced? Were there community resources that could be brought to patients to help them recover? The essentiality of knowing people as they relate to their environment and their mutual relationship goes beyond medical and hospital social work. It is the core of all social work practice. Consistent with and within the context of the person-in-environment, schools of social work prepare social workers, stressing the need for the medical social worker to understand the patient population and their health problems, the organizational setting, the community, intervention modalities and methods of research and program evaluation. Understanding the patient population and health problems includes being familiar with the usual path, treatment and management of a particular illness. This knowledge facilitates the engagement, assessment, planning, cooperation and overall communication with the patient and family members. In addition, it allows the social worker to interact knowledgeably with the other healthcare professionals with whom it is necessary to communicate on behalf of the patient. Understanding the organizational setting facilitates interdisciplinary teamwork and informal advocacy on behalf of the patient. Knowledge of the community allows the social worker at ease in linking patients to resources and facilitating referrals to other health-related programs that will aid the patient. Understanding specific treatment modalities and intervention approaches allows the social worker to meaningfully interact with patients and family members in the role of counselor and confidante. This skill enables the social worker to connect with the patient or family member to address emotional concerns and help the patient resolve problems related to the medical condition. Social workers are trained to be able to do research in any work setting. The social worker's ability to design and conduct research keeps social work vital and responsive to patient needs while documenting new areas of knowledge and understanding. Research on existing programs, especially those that reinforce interdisciplinary cooperation, is vital to serving patients' and family members' needs (Cowles, 2000).

Collaboration: The Interdisciplinary Teamwork

Collaboration occurs when a group of multiple professional experts participate in providing services to the clients. Collaboration is a complex and dynamic process that occurs when two or more healthcare providers cooperate and assist one another in the service of a patient or family member. Collaboration takes place between and among the various components of the healthcare team, also called the interdisciplinary team. The rationale for collaboration and interdisciplinary teamwork is that multidisciplinary knowledge and skills need to be put in and applied to best serve the patient and family. The interdisciplinary team may comprise physicians, nurses, social workers, physical therapists, psychiatrists, nutritionists and others who may be offering care to the patient. The unit or service within the hospital dictates the exact make-up of the interdisciplinary team. The functions of such teams include shared assessment of patient problems and needs, exchange of relevant information, team teaching of staff, development of intervention plans, ethical decision-making, delegation of tasks and responsibilities and evaluation of outcome (Cowles, 2000). Collaboration of this type requires a high degree of cooperation to be successful, with each participant knowing that they have something to contribute and that the contribution will be recognized in the decision-making about the patient. Collaboration has the potential to work well in a medical unit, but it is not without potential difficulties. Because the goal is to bring together different professions to address the needs of one patient, it is acknowledged that different professions bring different attitudes, values, skills and service orientations to the deliberations regarding what may be best for the patient (Rehr, Blumenfield, and Rosenberg, 1998).

Relevance of Medical Social Work

Bhore Committee (1946) recommended the training and appointment of social workers in hospital settings. In 1999, the Medical Council of India laid down minimum requirements to start medical colleges for 50-250 MBBS admissions per year, which has been amended from time to time. As per the latest guidelines, the above-mentioned medical colleges shall appoint certain numbers of medical and psychiatric social workers in the departments of community medicine, rural training health center, urban training health center, obstetrics and gynecology, pediatrics, psychiatry and physical medicine and rehabilitation. Over the years, the functioning of district hospitals has not been up to the mark as far as their availability, accessibility and quality issues are concerned. In order to provide comprehensive secondary healthcare services, which are based on standards of quality healthcare, responsiveness and sensitivity to the needs of the population of the district, a set of norms have been recommended for the district hospitals by the government, which is called as Indian Public Health Standards. These standards provide a benchmark to assess the functional state of hospitals. Henceforth, the district hospitals are expected to provide certain essential services such as clinical services, diagnostic services, ancillary services and administrative services. Medical Social Work has been incorporated as an "essential ancillary and support service" under IPHS. District hospitals shall appoint a certain number of social workers for hospitals having varied bed strength. Further, trained social workers have been appointed to various national health programmes run by the government.

Social Work Response to Pandemics

Pandemics impact not only the physical health of patients but also have far reaching effect on the social economic and psychological domains of their lives. Social workers have been instrumental in assisting pandemic-affected patients on the psychosocial and economic fronts. Emergency and pandemic events are known to have a wide-reaching psychological impact. These psychological impacts can include but are not limited to, emergency and pandemic-related distress (i.e., fear of death, post-traumatic stress disorder, diffused post-traumatic stress, future-oriented anxiety, grief), the physical isolation of people, families or communities resulting in non-pathologic distress and/or mental health problems among a small minority, worsening pre-existing issues (i.e., severe mental disorder, alcohol abuse) and humanitarian aid related problems i.e., anxiety about food distribution, etc. (IASC, 2007, 2015).

Epidemics are health emergencies that have a significant impact on people's lives, cause large numbers of fatalities and injuries, and lead to fear of infection, thus jeopardizing the safety and well-being of the community. The psychosocial impact of these events can exceed the ability of individuals and communities to manage them and can cause high levels of distress, which can persist long after the end of the outbreak (Johal et al., 2016). For instance, studies on the psychosocial effects of the SARS pandemic have shown a higher level of depression among those who were affected (Ko et al., 2006). The same is true of the psychosocial impacts of the Ebola outbreak and the Nipah virus (Van Bortel et al., 2016; Zacharias et al., 2019). Radhakrishnan C. et al., in their study on the psychosocial impacts of quarantine among survivors of the Nipah virus infection, mentioned that quarantine and isolation have several psychosocial implications for patients, families, workplaces and communities. During the isolation period, patients with NiV reported feelings of fear, isolation, boredom, anger and worry about the impact of quarantine and infection on family and friends. The discovery of a higher number of close contacts of NiV diagnosed individuals made the public more fearful. Healthcare workers were adversely affected by the fear of infection and the fear of infecting family, friends, colleagues and colleagues.

Survivors of pandemics report fear of death, stigmatization by the community and in some cases, discrimination and violence. Contacts and carers experience anxiety, grief and stigmatization. Although most survivors and carers display a wide range of distress reactions, some of them experience diagnosable impact on the community stigma and/or isolation, community and cultural disruption, loss of trust (for example, in health services), breakdown of community fabric, loss of support/coping resources, drop in income generation within the community travel and work restrictions, loss of family/ community members, collapse of businesses, impact on the world stigma, discrimination and guilt towards specific communities (because of fear of infection) and decreased interaction with areas affected. On the other hand, pre-existing social problems such as poverty, economic disparities, belonging to a marginalized group, political subjugation, extreme income loss, family separation, social network disruption, loss of community structure, loss of resources and trust and so on, can also have a psychological impact. In addition, humanitarian aid can also have a social and economic impact, such as undermining community structures or existing support mechanisms. While an emergency may affect masses, it is also likely to affect certain groups, such as women and children, elderly people, the poor, etc. (IASC, 2015; Van Bortel et al., 2016).

Social work is a humanitarian profession with a focus on helping individuals, groups and communities to improve or restore their capacity for social functioning and thereby creating favorable social conditions to achieve the common social good. Its primary purpose is to serve people directly and at the same time, make social institutions responsive to people. Social work values are based on the fundamental principles of service, social justice, community integrity and the dignity and worth of an individual. Professional social work played a crucial role in providing support and relief to the Covid-affected families and communities, especially when the pandemic peaked. In India and globally, professional social workers extended their services alongside doctors, health workers, police and other frontline workers.

Social work response to the wave of the pandemic can be broken down into several interventions namely raising awareness of COVID-19 related behaviors; providing personal hygiene, food and other relief supplies to the affected families; extending psychosocial counseling support; providing essential information on COVID-19 testing, vaccines, helpdesks, quarantine centers, oxygen supplies and entitlement documents; managing helpdesks; managing quarantines and centers; assisting in contact tracing; organizing COVID-19 camps; collaborating with governmental and non-governmental agencies; working with CSR programs; working with individual initiatives at local level; channeling local philanthropy and own resources to meet the needs of the distressed families; reaching out to the invisible and hard to reach populations; recruiting, training and providing volunteers and social workers for COVID-19; responding to COVID-19 affected families; establishing new initiatives; assisting government and other implementing bodies in the systematic response to the relief activities (Prasad et al., 2022).

The COVID-19 pandemic caused by SARS-CoV-2 first appeared in China in December 2019 and thereafter, was rapidly advanced into a global disease (Gupta et al., 2020). As of 14 June 2023, the disease has been confirmed in 767,984,989 individuals, including 6,943,390 deaths reported to the World Health Organization. The second wave of COVID-19 unprecedentedly devastated our lives. The majority of nations were shocked and unprepared for the pandemic catastrophe in 2021. India witnessed the worst second wave of the Delta virus, resulting in high infection rates and enormous loss of human life. According to the UNICEF India COVID-19 Pandemic Situation Report (May 2021), the month of May 2021 saw more than 3 cases per second and nearly 3 deaths per minute at the height of the surge of the virus (Prasad et al., 2022).

Due to the pandemic, the manufacturing industry came to a halt, causing severe shortages of various essential supplies everywhere. As the infection is transmitted by droplets, there was growing demand for personal protective gear like face masks, hand sanitizers, goggles, face shields, oxygen cylinders and anti-viral drugs. The corona virus outbreak resulted in the closedown of outpatient services and elective surgeries, with in-patient admissions happening only through an emergency, which escalated its workload many times. MSWs played a key role in patient coordination and their transfers to COVID units, availability of face masks and other PPE gear, transfer of dead bodies, grief counseling and help to poor patients. Gupta et al.

have described the contribution of social work professionals in the pandemic situation in the following words:

> AIIMS hospital was designated as one of the COVID19 hospitals by Ministry of Health and Family welfare, Govt. of India. It had its own requirements, challenges and indeed the opportunities to improve its system & processes. Keeping these in consideration, a team of 06 MSSOs were posted round the clock in the emergency department to help, guide and facilitate for specials requirements of the patients. Patients who had their planned surgeries scheduled and were in Delhi, the MSSO helped them in getting accommodation to stay in the Vishram Sadans of AIIMS. The team of MSSOs counselled the inmates of our Vishram Sadans (both patients and their attendants) on the aspects of hand hygiene, respiratory etiquettes and social distancing. The time period of first lock down w.e.f. 24th March 2020 to 14th April 2020 was the most challenging one as it adversely affected the various supply chains of crucial items. At this juncture, the infantry of our MSSOs took the lead. They tapped the philanthropists, industrialists and entrepreneurs of society. They coordinated with them and arranged for the special permissions required to be given to their industrial units to open and manufacture the masks and other PPE items. Finally, the delivery of these items from the industrial units to our hospital also posed a lot of administrative challenges at the various border check points during the lock down for which the permissions were arranged by the MSSOs. Through their tenacious efforts and duty beyond the call, they managed to arrange PPE items in huge quantities. A unique requirement voiced by our security guards manning the various peripheral security check posts on the campus came to us during these times regarding the bar soaps if could be made available to them as they had access to water but needed soaps at these posts. Without any delay, through the personal efforts of MSSO, the soaps were made available to them through donations in 24 hours time. (p. 611)

MSWs have also been actively engaged in helping COVID-infected patients whose contacts were unreachable or whose relatives were not coming to receive them after the recovery or who were unattended/abandoned/unknown. For this, medical social workers coordinated with the hospital administration, patient relatives, police and NGOs to rehabilitate such patients.

According to Kodom (2022), medical social workers are engaged in preparing and monitoring policies that pertain to the treatment of clients in mental health facilities. As mental health issues intensify in the pandemic situation, medical social workers identify community and environmental factors that impede the mental health of individuals. They provide psychosocial analysis of the needs of patients and offer opportunities to waive the medical bills of vulnerable patients. In addition, they explore and address issues related to the abuse of children and domestic violence, which usually cause health problems during the pandemic. Since medical social workers are competent in providing counseling, they have used this skill with other allied healthcare teams to deal with the psychological and social consequences of the pandemic. They have been involved in developing a therapeutic relationship in counseling with individuals or families to help them recover from illness and post-discharge care and address the issues of addiction related to the pandemic. Because of the increased demand for healthcare facilities due to the pandemic, they refer patients to the appropriate institutions for follow-up care, helping in case management and promoting healthcare. Hospital social workers are in a better position to take on frontline roles, helping to provide optimal healthcare and connecting individuals to services and resources at nursing homes, clinics and other places of care.

Sivakumar (2020) observed that corona-suspected individuals undergo great emotional distress. The medical social worker provided information and counsel led the tested individuals and their families. At times, the situation became very intricate; for instance, the mother of two young kids became positive, and the father had to care for them, which he had never done before. Likewise, an elderly couple was tested, and the wife turned positive and was admitted to hospital. The husband felt deserted to handle his life alone, and a couple was admitted and had to leave their little kid with the neighbor as no close relative was available. Here, social work intervention is desirable to address the complex issues of the patient and their families.

Okafor (2021) has also described that social work services are essential in emergencies and pandemics. Several COVID-19 survivors may need palliative or non-curative care. Trained social workers can provide the best compassionate care to these individuals. The role of professional social workers is not only within health facilities but also within poor households that have insufficient or no medical insurance. They should promote kinship care and support services for the welfare of older people and arrange safe spaces for children/minors whose parents/guardians expired in the pandemic.

Despite its vital role in healthcare, the progress in medical social work has been very slow. The requirement of the profession is not solemnly realized by those concerned with the health of society. The policymakers, the planners, the government, the health team and the NGOs at large are not yet fully satisfied about the need for social work in health settings. More specifically, the response from the planners is also not supportive, as it is found in many committee reports such as the Mudaliar Committee (GOI, 1961), Shrivastava Committee (GOI, 1975), etc. In practice, many hospitals and medical colleges do not employ the required number of social workers. Private hospitals seem more or less reluctant to appoint medical social workers.

There are some reasons for the meager development of the hospital social work practice. In Indian hospital settings, the qualifications, functions and duties of doctors, nurses and other auxiliary personnel have been clearly defined. But for social workers, neither the functions are identified nor are the qualifications recognized. Even the social workers themselves and the medical team are not able to identify the numerous roles of social workers in healthcare settings. Consequently, they receive less acceptance and low status in the medical team. In hospitals and related health institutions, tangible outcomes are of great value, whereas the results of social workers' interventions are usually intangible because they deal with the psychosocial issues of the patients. Many times, their contribution is not assessed adequately by the administrators and the medical team. In many hospitals, the social workers function as single workers. Mostly, they are involved in routine and monotonous non-professional duties, which hamper their motivation to work effectively. The remunerations of the medico-social workers are comparatively low among the members of the health team. In addition to this, there are several other problems, which also affect the quality of the services. There is a slack of comprehensive studies to understand the practice of social work in hospital settings in the country.

For all the above practical reasons, the study entitled "Status of Professional Social Workers Employed in Major Hospitals in Delhi" has been undertaken. It is expected that the findings of the research will throw light on the functions, application of social work methods, service conditions and extent of job satisfaction of medical social workers in hospitals of Delhi.

References

Anand, A.C. (2019). "Indian healthcare at crossroads: Deteriorating doctor-patient relationship". *The National Medical Journal of India,* 32(1), 41-45.

Bartlett, H. (1961). *Social Work Practice in the Health Field.* New York: National Association of Social Workers.

Berkman, B., and Volland, P. (1997). "Health Care Practice Overview". *Encyclopedia of Social Work* (Vol. 19, pp. 143-49).

Cowles, L.A.F. (2003). *Social Work in the Health Field: A Care Perspective* (2nd ed.). Routledge.

Cowles, L.A.F. (2000). *Social work in the Health Field.* New York: Haworth Press.

Grace, M. (1979). *The role of non-professionals in the treatment of the mentally ill patients in mental hospitals* (unpublished thesis). Tata Institute of Social Sciences, Mumbai.

Gupta, A., Sodhi, J., Shekhar, B.R., and Sharma, D.K. (2020). "Medical Social Service Officers and their Contribution in COVID-19 Pandemic". *Indian J Comm Health*, 32(3), 610-12.

Inter-Agency Standing Committee. (2007). *IASC guidelines on mental health and psychosocial support in emergency settings.* Geneva: Author.

Ko, C-H., Yen, Ju-Yu., Yang, M-J. (2006). "Psychosocial impact among the public of the severe acute respiratory syndrome epidemic in Taiwan". *Psychiatry Clin Neurosci,* 60, 397-403. https://doi.org/10.1111/j.1440-1819.2006.01522.x.

Kodom, R.B. (2022). "The role of social work in the healthcare settings during the COVID-19 pandemic in Africa". *International Social Work,* 66(5), 1567-72.

McMahon, B.K. (1958). "Medical social work as an integrative activity in hospital practice". In Dora Goldstine (Ed.). *Readings in the theory and practice of medical social work.* Chicago: The University of Chicago Press.

Okafor, A. (2021). "Role of the social worker in the outbreak of pandemics (A case of COVID-19)." *Cogent Psychology,* 8(1), 1-7.

Prasad, D.B., Keshri, A., and Deshwal, S. (2022). *Professional Social Work Response to COVID-19 Affected Families in India* (1st ed.). NAPSWI.

Radhakrishnan, C., Sankar, U.V., Rajendran, V.R., et al. (2021). "Psychosocial impacts of quarantine among survivors of the Nipah virus infection: A qualitative study". *Journal of Global Health Reports,* 5, e2021092. https://doi.org/10.29392/001c.28993

Rehr, H., Blumenfield, S., and Rosenberg, G. (1998). "Collaboration and consultation: Key social work roles in health care". In H. Rehr, G. Rosenberg, and S. Blumenfield (Eds.), *Creative social work in healthcare* (pp. 93-99). New York: Springer.

Rock, B. (2002). "Social work in health care for the 21st century: The bio-psychosocial model". In A.R. Roberts and G.J. Greene (Eds.), *Social workers' desk reference* (pp. 10-15). New York: Oxford University Press.

Sheps, C.G. (1973). *Trends in health care administration: A managerial perspective* (pp. 21-23). Philadelphia: Lippincott.

Sivakumar, C. (2020). "COVID-19 Social Work Scope and Intervention in a Tertiary Care Hospital". *Advanced Journal of Social Science,* 7(1), 92-95.

Van Bortel, T., Basnayake, A., Wurie, F., Jambai, M., Koroma, A., Muana, A., Hann, K., Eaton, J., Martin, S., Nellums, L. (2016). "Psychosocial effects of an Ebola outbreak at individual, community and international levels". *Bulletin of World Health Organization.* https://doi.org/10.2471/blt.15.158543

Zacharias, L., Harikrishnan, U., Jayakumar, C., Sekar, K. (2019). Psychosocial perspective of Nipah virus outbreak in Kerala, India. 10.17354/ijss/2018/30

2

Evolution, Scope and Functions of Hospital Social Work

Medical social work popped up in the Indian scenario half a century later as compared to the contemporary Western world. At the time of independence, infant and maternal mortality and crude death rates were very high in the country. The life span was only 32.4 years for males and 31.7 years for females. The death rate of mothers at the time of delivery was 20/1000 live births. Abortion, miscarriage, toxemia and sepsis were major causes of death during pregnancy. Malaria, tuberculosis and leprosy were the main public health hazards. In addition, there were the enormous problems of undernutrition and malnutrition. Health facilities, both curative and preventive, were unsatisfactory (Sinha, 1980). Evidently, deficiencies in delivering health services can only be overcome through effective health planning. Hence, the Government of India constituted the Health Survey and Development Committee, popularly known as the Bhore Committee, to study the then-existing health conditions and institutions in the country and make suggestions for further development. The committee, in its report (1946), recommended the training and appointment of trained social workers in hospital settings.

This committee enumerated the following functions for hospital social workers: (a) making an enquiry about the environmental factors affecting the patients, (b) helping patients to follow the treatment regimen, (c) assisting patients to overcome barriers in the treatment and recovery, (d) linkages with the community agencies, (e) health education and health promotion, (f) resource mobilization, and (g) look over the abuse of hospital resources. The committee members met the then Director of Tata Institute of Social Sciences and firmly emphasized the training of social workers in hospital settings. Consequently, specialized training in the field of medical and psychiatric social work was commenced in 1948 under the leadership of Dr. G.R. Banerjee, who had undergone training in the U.S.A. (Marulasiddaiah and Sherif, 1981).[1]

The J.J. Hospital of Mumbai recruited the first professional social worker in 1946. In Delhi, the first medical social worker was appointed in 1950 in Lady Irwin Hospital. Thereafter, other hospitals gradually began to appoint them to their hospital staff (Seal, 1974). The Medical Council of India (now repealed) was set up in 1934 to conserve consistency in the standards of medical education, acknowledging medical qualifications of medical colleges, registrations of doctors and mutual acceptance of medical qualifications with foreign institutions. In 1999, the council laid down minimum requirements to start medical colleges for 50-250 MBBS admissions per year, which has been amended from time to time. As per the latest guidelines, the above-mentioned medical colleges shall appoint certain numbers of medical and psychiatric social workers in the departments of community medicine, rural training health center, urban training health center, obstetrics and gynecology, pediatrics, psychiatry and physical medicine and rehabilitation.

In our country, public health services are imparted at three levels, i.e., primary, secondary and tertiary healthcare.

---

1. Appointment of medical social workers is a mandatory requirement for hospitals. As NCT of Delhi is a hub of healthcare facilities, therefore, an attempt was made to understand medical social work practice in Delhi hospitals by conducting personal interviews with professional social workers employed by these hospitals. The author undertook extensive literature review on the subject and used a structured and pre-tested interview schedule to collect the data from 145 hospital social workers. The data was analysed on SPSS version 20 and presented with tables and graphs.

Secondary-level health services are dispensed through district hospitals to the people of the district. While delivering healthcare services at this level, district hospitals are required to ensure participation of the geographical population and cooperation of various agencies with similar health concerns so that the health services being provided are effective and affordable for both urban as well as rural populations in the district. Over the years, the functioning of district hospitals has not been up to the mark as far as its availability, accessibility and quality issues are concerned. To provide comprehensive secondary healthcare services, which are based on standards of quality healthcare, responsiveness and sensitivity to the needs of the population of the district, a set of norms have been recommended for the district hospitals by the government, which is called as Indian Public Health Standards. These standards provide a benchmark to assess the functional state of hospitals. Henceforth, the district hospitals are expected to provide certain essential services such as 46 clinical services, diagnostic services, ancillary services and administrative services. Further, the IPHS has been categorized in accordance with the bed strength of the hospitals, i.e., norms for 100-500 bedded district hospitals. Medical Social Work has been incorporated as an "essential ancillary and support service" under IPHS, and district hospitals shall appoint 2 to 6 social workers for hospitals having 100 to 500-bed strength.

There is an enormous burden of mental disorders and a scarcity of qualified professionals in the field of mental health. With the aim of meeting the needs of mental healthcare services Government of India launched the National Mental Health Programme in 1982. In 1996, the District Mental Health Program was introduced, which was re-strategized in 2003 and two components—modernization of state mental hospitals and up-gradation of psychiatric wings of medical colleges/general hospitals, became part of the program. Again, in 2009, Scheme A & B for manpower development was included in the program. Under NMHP, the government has been providing financial assistance to hospitals/medical colleges to appoint psychiatric social workers and run academic courses in psychiatric social work.

In 1992, the Indian Government launched the National AIDS Control Programme. Under this program, an autonomous organization named National AIDS Control Organization (NACO) was set up to implement an exhaustive program to combat HIV/AIDS in the country. A wide range of activities of NACP are carried out via Integrated Counseling and Testing Centers, PPTCT Programmes, Anti-Retroviral Treatment Centers, STD/RTI Clinics and Blood Banks, mainly located in public hospitals. NACO has framed operational guidelines for the above-mentioned centers, which make it mandatory to appoint counselors with a degree preferably in social work. As a result, a number of professional social workers are employed in the field of HIV/AIDS.

Blood Bank is an essential patient care service of the hospital, and to provide adequate and safe blood/blood products to patients is the responsibility of the concerned hospital. According to NACO, voluntary blood donation and availability of safe blood has increased over the years, yet, there are gaps and challenges in ensuring the availability and accessibility of safe blood to all those who need it. The Government of India constituted an Expert Working Group to review and recommend revised norms for Blood Banks in the country. The expert working group submitted its report in 2017 and recommended having one to four medical social workers/counselors for blood banks with annual blood collection ranging from 5000 to >50,000 units. The working group also recommended two medical social workers/counselors as an additional minimum staff required to collect 50-120 blood donors for the outdoor blood donation camp.

Two national-level professional bodies ISPSW and IAMSWP have been making concentrated efforts to promote medical and psychiatric social work in India. Indian Society of Psychiatric Social Work was set up in 1970 in the Department of Psychiatric Social Work, Central Institute of Psychiatry, Ranchi. Later, the nomenclature of the society was changed to the Indian Society of Professional Social Work in 1988. ISPSW aims to bring social work professionals together to deliberate and develop conceptual frameworks and indigenous social work practices.

ISPSW conducts an annual conference and publishes the *National Journal of Social Work*. In 2009, the All India Association of Medical Social Work Professionals (AIAMSWP) was set up to promote the standards and status of social work professionals and safeguard the interests of professional social workers in healthcare in the country. The association conducts annual seminars/conferences, publishes the *Indian Journal of Health Social Work* and further aims to establish practice guidelines, organize regular workshops/training programs and develop a network of medical and psychiatric social work departments.

Globally, numerous studies have been undertaken to understand social work practice in healthcare settings. In the study, "Perceived workforce challenges among clinical social workers in hematopoietic cell transplantation programs", Ferguson et al. (2018, pp. 1063-68) have attempted to know the structure of social work services at transplant centers, understand the role of Hematopoietic Cell Transplant (HCT) clinical social workers, study job satisfaction, find out difficulties in fulfilling the needs of patients and families and explore the capacity of and issues in ensuring adequate social work staffing for future HCT needs. A web-based survey comprising 34 items was administered to 159 HCT social workers. The respondents were recruited from US transplant centers and professional associations' memberships, i.e., the Association of Oncology Social Work (AOSW) and the Association of Pediatric Oncology Social Workers (APOSW). About 90 respondents from 76 transplant centers participated. The results revealed that social workers spent an average (61.3%) of their time on clinical social work tasks. Non-clinical activities, such as referral for financial help, application to government entitlement programs, and case management related to discharge planning, were carried out daily by more than one-third of the participants. More than 80 percent informed being very contented or satisfied as an HCT social worker. The competence to provide psychosocial care from assessment through transplantation and survivorship (transplant trajectory), the opportunity to help patients and families in life-threatening situations and feeling valued as an important member of the team were the top three most satisfying aspects of being an HCT clinical social worker. Insufficient time to offer clinical social work services, the emotional drain of treating chronically ill and dying patients and low salary were selected as the top three least satisfying aspects of being a clinical social worker. The most common difficulties were sequencing competing patient needs, overcoming financial hardships for uninsured or underinsured patients, dedicating time for patient care divided across multiple programs, and having a heavy workload.

In the study, "Social work student and practitioner roles in integrated care settings". *American Journal of Preventive Medicine*, Fraher, Richmond, and Zerden (2018) identified the functions of social workers in integrated medical and behavior healthcare settings. MSW trainees and their field guides were selected for the study. The researchers observed that the most frequent functions of social workers included implementing cultural competency, documenting in the electronic health record, dealing with patient's social determinants of health and participating in multidisciplinary healthcare. Respondents were least likely to be engaged in case conferences, assessments, brief interventions and referral to treatment, use step-by-step care to decide the necessary level of treatment, conduct functional assessments of life skills and use behavioral modification and problem-solving therapy.

In the study, "Overcoming barriers to eye care: Patient response to a medical social worker in a glaucoma service", *Journal of Community Health*, Fudemberg et al. (2016) have described the results of a retrospective chart review of 50 glaucoma patients who were referred to a medical social worker between 5 January 2015 and 31 June 2015 in an OPD clinic of an urban eye hospital. Clinical and demographic data, as well as the data on a quality-of-care questionnaire, were collected for each patient. Patients rated their interaction with the medical social worker as highly positive (mean = 4.75, 5-point Likert scale), and nearly 90 percent of patients showed interest in future contact with the social worker. The majority of patients (61.1%) informed that the social worker supported them in resolving the issues they were facing, assisted them (70.6%)

in seeing their ophthalmologist, and aided them (69.7%) inappropriately handling their illness. Reported barriers to glaucoma care were emotional turmoil, expenses of office visits and medications, absence of medical insurance, transportation, poor medication compliance, disturbance in routine activities, follow-up adherence and language. The study recommends that MSW could play a significant role in supporting patients with glaucoma disease to overcome challenges to treatment and helping in disease management.

In the study, "Social work in hospitals in Slovakia: Current working conditions and difficulties in the view of the professionals", Slana et al. (2016) attempted to ascertain the crucial factors responsible for the job performance and job satisfaction of medical social workers. The leading factors that considerably decided their work situation were the non-existence of statutory guidelines that give only a little orientation to social workers, organizational structures that are not ready to completely endorse social work as an integrated component of healing processes, hospital cultures which do not encourage inter-professional teamwork and challenges in coordinating patients discharge and post-hospital follow up. The above situations create obstacles in social workers' interventions in hospitals and compel them to keep on advocating their own status and strengths.

In the study, "Bouncers, brokers and glue: The self-described roles of social workers in urban hospitals", Craig and Muskat (2013) highlighted the activities of hospital social workers. Seven focus groups (n = 65) were selected for the study and facilitated in hospitals serving adults, children and patients with medical and mental health issues. One more focus group was invited to a conference on social work in healthcare. The researchers enquired from social workers about their own conception of the roles they played in medical settings. Seven major themes emerged from the analysis that mentioned social workers as bouncers, janitors, glues, brokers, firefighters, jugglers and challengers. These roles included an array of tasks and responsibilities wherein social workers often acted as a link between patients, families, medical teams and internal and external services.

In the study, "Hospital social work: Contemporary roles and professional activities", *Social Work in Health Care*, Judd and Sheffield (2010) collected data from 377 social workers employed in different hospitals in the U.S.A. The study presented that acute medical services (surgery services, ICU/CCU, orthopedics, transplant, inpatient physical rehabilitation and oncology), aging services, children's services and ancillary services (home health, outpatient dialysis emergency room) were the service lines which consumed the majority of respondents' time. Discharge planning, counseling, crisis intervention, bioethics, evidence-based practice and income-generating projects were identified as the major activities of medical social workers.

In the study, "A discussion of professional issues of hospital social workers in Saudi Arabia", Albrithen and Yalli (2013) presented certain issues pertaining to social work practice in hospital settings through empirical research. More than half of the participants in the study were male. They had experience of up to thirty years as hospital social workers. Most of the respondents held a bachelor's degree. The responses indicated two kinds of employment of social workers in Saudi hospitals—administrative and professional. Data also revealed that social workers may work on three shifts. Permanent posts were held by 65.8 percent of participants, while the remaining 34.2 percent worked on short-term contracts. The results of the study illustrated that limited skills and insufficient training were the perceived handicaps in the effective role performance of hospital social workers.

In the study, "Hospital social workers in Saudi Arabia: Characteristics and functions", Albrithen and Yalli (2015) highlighted the several job responsibilities of hospital social workers. The data revealed that daily rounds in hospital units, assessment of psychological and social factors of illness, administrative duties, consoling and psychotherapy, referral, research, advocacy, health education, training, consultation, discharge planning, budgeting, fundraising, community organization, capacity building and post hospitalization follow-up were the major activities undertaken by medico-social workers in the country.

In the study, "A pilot survey of social work services in pediatric primary care programs in urban teaching hospitals", Meyers, Bailly, Rheaume, Riley, and DeChillo (2001) conducted the study to decide the current status of social work involvement in pediatric primary care clinics in urban teaching hospitals. 80 percent of practices informed of having on-site social work services. 95 percent of respondents viewed social work services in pediatric primary care to be significant.

In the study, "Can physicians' admission evaluation of patients' status help to identify patients requiring social work interventions?", Hou, Hollenberg and Charlson (2001) attempted to study the utility of physicians' initial clinical assessments in selecting patients admitted from their homes who subsequently require social work intervention for discharge planning in an academic hospital. Findings revealed that aged patients, sicker and less functional, had higher requirements for social work intervention ($P < 0.001$). New nursing home placement patients were older and had worse function ($P < 0.001$). Total expenditure of hospital stay was estimated by discharge orders. It was concluded that early discharge planning has often been thought of as a viable mechanism to diminish the cost of hospitalization and reduce the length of stay. Age and evaluation of functional status by the doctor at admission may provide early discovery of patients who need social work intervention.

The survey report presented by Cowles and Lefcowitz (1995) highlights the standpoint of doctors, nurses, and social workers regarding the role of medical social workers in dealing with patients' health problems. All three groups, especially doctors and nurses, opined counseling services as a social worker's task if the client was a family/relative rather than the patient and when the objective was to overcome social/environmental issues of the client rather than to support or modify the individual. Also, all three groups, especially doctors and nurses, perceived the social difficulties of patients, more than emotional or behavioral ones, as a field of distinctive social work intervention. In contrast to previous study findings, doctors and nurses did not want to exclude social workers in hospitals from counseling patients and dealing with psychosocial obstacles.

In the study, "Interdisciplinary expectations of the medical social worker in the hospital setting", Cowles and Lefcowitz (1992) did a survey. Around 500 physicians, nurses and social workers working in four general hospitals participated in a mailed questionnaire survey designed to compare inter-professional expectations of the medical social worker's role in the hospital. As was hypothesized, doctors and nurses assumed the exclusive role of the social worker to be more confined to working with families, sorting out social-environmental problems and making referrals. Generally, physicians and nurses do not dissent with medical social workers on what social workers expect to do in the hospital setting; rather, they do not agree more on what social workers expect to be their distinctive role. Moreover, it does not seem that other groups decline either the bio-psychosocial model or social worker expertise. Instead, these groups view the special attention of the medical social worker in the hospital as building the social support and resources of the patient, looking at the patient's family as a unit of that support system. These other groups may be reluctant to the person-in-environment perspective of hospital social work.

In the study, "Clinical social work in a medical setting", Bergman, Contro, and Zivetz (1984) using a case vignette and discussion, elaborates on two distinct activities of the clinical social worker practicing in a medical setting: (i) assisting patient, family and staff to recognize the emotional impact of physical illness and (ii) aiding a family to acknowledge that there may be no organic etiology for a symptom, and it may be psychogenic in origin. Difficulties in performing these functions, as well as reasons for the social worker being in an apt position to combine clinical and psychological data into a coherent and practical treatment plan are discussed.

In the study, "Healthcare social work in Nigeria", Okoye (2019) has mentioned that counseling for psychologically depressed patients, palliative care, soliciting financial assistance for indigent patients, rehabilitating deserted patients, home visits and follow-up, creating contributory fund projects and encouraging blood donors were the major areas of social work intervention in healthcare.

In the study, "Establishing the place of health social work", Sarah, Christina, and Browne (2019) put forward that by virtue of their holistic understanding of social problems, social workers keep the knowledge and skills that are essential to identify and address social determinants of health, which has presented a long-time challenge in healthcare settings. There is enough evidence to demonstrate that social factors not only influence the health condition of people but also their ability to access and benefit from the healthcare system. Through this unique contribution, our profession can advance a more socially oriented model of health by sharing and expanding our expertise in five primary domains: (1) escalating screening and prevention, (2) handling socio-economic issues in healthcare, (3) ameliorating care management and coordination, (4) encouraging interventions adapted to vulnerable groups, and (5) aiding successful care conversions.

In the study, "Social work services utilization by children with medical complexity", *Maternal and Child Health Journal*, Coquillette et al. compared hospital-wide social work services utilization by medically complex children with non-medically complex children to inform the evolution of family-centred care models which support these vulnerable patients and families. A tertiary children's hospital was used to compare children with medical complexity aged 0-17 (N = 564) with age and sex-matched non-CMC (N = 1128). The main outcome measures were the proportion of patients who used social work services and the mean number of hours of services provided per patient. A greater percentage of CMC (60.3%) utilised social work services than non-CMC (18.9%). CMC used more hours per child (5.50 h/child) as compared to non-CMC (0.69 h/child). In multivariate analysis, medical complexity was associated with 6.23-fold greater odds of using social work services (95% CI 4.94-7.85) and with 8.07 times more hours of services per child (95% CI 6.30-10.34), independent of primary health insurance, age or sex. This data proves that CMC utilises significantly more social work services in hospital settings. This must be kept in mind while designing proactive medical home models to provide high-quality family-centred care for this population, and further research is needed to elucidate the factors that drive this utilization.

In the study, "Hospital Social Work in Australia: Emerging Trends or More of the Same?", Cleak and Turczynski (2014) mentioned that social work in healthcare has been in place for over 100 years and is one of the biggest social work practice areas. Over the years, demographic changes, an increase in the aged population, improvement in longevity rates, explosion of chronic illness, together with the rapidly escalating cost of healthcare, have raised serious challenges for acute hospitals and health social workers. This article reviews the Australian healthcare system and policies, particularly the public hospital system. It also examines the latest hospital social work roles, including the continued role in discharge planning and enlarging responsibility for upcoming client problems, such as patient complexity, legal and care issues. The article concludes with a discussion of evolving issues and challenges encountered by health social workers to ensure that social work remains adaptable within this practice context.

In the study, "Social work in health care: An international perspective", Pockett and Beddoe (2017) critically examined several aspects of globalization, the relationship between health disparities and social inequalities and the implications for social work practice. Giles suggested developing a 'health equality imagination'. However, the challenge for social work practitioners on a day-to-day basis was how to include such an imagination into the practice. A number of recommended approaches for greater involvement in dealing with health inequalities in social work practice, education and research are also presented. In mitigating health inequalities and inequities, it is argued that social work practice must be underpinned by socially inclusive and empowering approaches. Social workers must frame their practice around the following key elements: (i) taking a holistic approach to people's well-being, assuming that threats to physical and mental health are likely to affect all the people with whom they work, (ii) working on the social determinants of health, (iii) confronting discrimination, violence, prejudice and stigma, (iv) keeping in mind the effect of health inequalities on the lives of individuals, groups and communities, (v) proactively participate in professional interest groups that link to global health networks, (vi) function inter-professionally assuring the role of these important perspectives, (vii) analyzing their work and positively informing it to others, and (viii) looking at health work as a domain for action and advocacy locally, nationally and internationally and most importantly, that the relevance and significance of these complexities should be reflected in their practice.

In the study, "Complex families, the social determinants of health and psychosocial interventions: Deconstruction of a day in the life of hospital social workers", B. Muskat et al. administered a cross-sectional survey to explore the needs of patients and interventions by social workers within a large urban Canadian paediatric hospital. This group of hospital social workers comprised staff that work in IPD and OPD of medical and mental health programs with patients with acute and chronic conditions. The most reported cost to families was medicines (50%), transportation (48%), medical supplies (26%), medical equipment (16%), nutritional supplements (16%), rehabilitation (12%), special programming (10%) and house alteration (2%). Education, accommodation, social inclusion and food security were the factors that added to the psychosocial complications for patients and families. The greatest social determinant of health risk factor reported in the sample was social inclusion (48%), followed by education (44%), housing (30%) and food security (23%). Social workers, most frequently, offered supportive counseling (44%), structured therapy (15%), education (11%), economic support (9%), evaluation (7%), providing resources (6%), advocacy (5%), transportation (1%) and planning (1%).

Social workers are experts in knowing, assessing and intervening in individual, family-related and practical issues that influence health. They are the only health professionals in the medical settings whose functions are closely connected to social health issues yet disconnected from the physical care of patients. The medical social worker is a specialist in the social dimension of health and a social doctor who has a role to play like any other specialist. MSWs emphasize either the psychological or social treatment, according to the nature of the problem, but consider both in their relation to the ailment and the treatment. Although social workers do not apply medical technology to treat patients, as do physicians, nurses and physical and occupational therapists, they do question the aim of technology, encourage communication, negotiate among participants and advocate for patients. By taking care outside the hospital and clinic into the community and the home, they add continuity and perspective to the medical plan. They offer effective professional services to the medical team.

Davis et al. (2004) undertook a quantitative study to understand the role of medical social workers and the specific activities performed by them in a public hospital in Australia. The results showed that apart from discharge planning, social assessment, counseling and liaison consumed most of their time. According to Albrithen and Yalli (2015), the predominant role of social work practitioners may entail offering direct clinical service via psychosocial work with individuals or with families and groups. Other roles include program planning, raising funds and budgeting. Yet another role consists of training and teaching, research and health education. Beder (2006) stated that medico-social workers took up tasks that comprised assessments of patients' social environment, guiding patients regarding the hospital stay and educating them about the potential impact of the diagnosis, helping patients to follow the treatment regimen and linkage to community agencies.

Social workers' activities comprise counseling (Cowles and Lefcowitz, 1995); surveillance, identifying and building community resources (Cowles and Lefcowitz, 1992); linkages between patients and resources (Guo and Company, 2007); coordination with medical teams (Green and Kulper, 1990; Albrithen and Yalli, 2015); documentation (NASW, 2005).

Okoye (2019) described the following functions for healthcare social workers: Counseling Services, Palliative Care, Soliciting Financial Assistance for Indigent Patients, Deportation of Deserted Patients, Home Visits and Follow-Up in Special Cases, Creating Contributory Fund Projects, Encouraging Blood Donor, Public sensitization toward public health, HIV/

AIDS and other related disease campaigns, Supervision of student generalist practitioners/social workers with regards to fieldwork practice and internships, Communication of policies and practices of the medical facility to patients and their support networks, Recommendation of policies and practices to the facility's management that will enhance the wellbeing of patients, Participation in ward rounds to ascertain the psychosocial conditions of patients and exchange ideas with other professionals, Provide friendship to patients and their support networks.

Ferguson et al. (2017) described that clinical social workers are social care experts who intervene to deal with the psychological, relational, monetary and logistical problems that come up during the hematopoietic cell transplantation (HCT) treatment and recovery process. Berkman (1996) enumerated the following tasks of hospital social workers: assisting patients and their families in managing the treatment plan, counseling and assisting the psychologically disturbed, helping in decision-making, educating about emotional issues, supporting in resolving behavioral issues, helping to find out and receive entitlement benefits, helping the healthcare team and offering risk management.

The present study identifies the following functions of hospital social workers:

Counseling

The World Health Organization has defined counseling as a mutual dialogue and interaction process aimed at building motivation to solve problems and facilitate decision-making. According to the United Nations Population Fund (UNFPA), counseling involves:

- A trained helper and one or more clients,
- A relationship based on acceptance and trust,
- A process that enables clients to better understand themselves and their social environment,
- A process that helps clients make future goals,
- A process that supports clients to gain the skills and courage to achieve these goals.

Counseling is one-to-one intercourse via purposeful interaction in which the counsellor assists the client in reaching a decision. This process requires active listening to people sharing their problems, an empathetic attitude and empowering them to bring about the solution to their problems. It is a helping rapport that enables a client to explore a personal problem, gain increased awareness of options than what they already keep in dealing with the problem, and make an informed decision about what to do about the problem. Counseling is also a process of exchanging information, sharing disturbed feelings and emotions that hamper social functioning. The client is unable to sort out their problem alone or with the existing social support.

Patient Counseling is defined as an individualized process encompassing guidance and joint problem-solving to support the patient in better management of the health problem. The purpose of counseling is to help patients handle their chronic disease by utilizing existing medical, social and financial resources. Patients are required to develop their own knowledge of the problem and how to manage it. A patient who is appropriately trained achieves a better quality of life, the illness stays under control, the treatment is persistent and hospital costs are reduced. According to Bor and Allen (2007), various issues and problems in medical settings like PTSD, coping and adjustment, pain management, pre and post-operative stress, HIV/AIDS, adjustment to chronic heart disease drug abuse, kidney failure, non-adherence to treatment, infertility, anxiety, etc. are handled by counseling. The counseling tasks as a major activity for hospital-based social work include supportive counseling to enhance the coping ability, counseling to alter attitudes and perceptions, and counseling to deal with social problems. Counseling helps a patient articulate their feelings about disability, roles and self-esteem. Further, the counselors can help patients understand terminologies and/or cope with problems, gaps or other alterations.

Overall, 93.1 percent of respondents in the study informed that their work profile encompasses counseling with patients on numerous issues. The findings indicate that there is not much difference in the percentage of respondents involved in counseling in all four age groups. An almost equal percentage of male and female respondents are providing counseling services to the patients and their families, and there is not much difference in the number of respondents involved in doing counseling in major hospital settings in terms of their level of education. Hence, it is concluded that most of the social workers in the hospitals of Delhi are involved in providing counseling services.

Psychosocial Study

Psychosocial study of patients involves gathering information about the patient, the family and other significant ones like the patient's living conditions, economic status, occupational status, support system, personal strengths, coping mechanisms, risk factors, community resources and so on. Such information helps the social worker and medical team to assess the patient's and family's needs in the process of treatment.

The physician responsible for the care of the patient must relate the social data to other findings in order to comprehend the interaction of the health and social situation. It should be readily accessible for his use. This may be accomplished either by filing the full social history or a summary of it with the medical chart or by conferences between physician and social worker. The interpretation of the social factors which the social worker can give may add much to the significance of the findings and focus attention on them at a time when they can be of the greatest value as a basis for a complete understanding of the patient and his resources and for outlining a plan of medical social treatment.

Social workers apply specific skills and knowledge to an evaluation process that acknowledges a person's emotional well-being and social context. While endorsing the influence of these factors, social workers can plan interventions in order to enhance patient's well-being and social functioning. During psychosocial study, they investigate the physical, emotional and sociological aspects of the client's problem. This comprises hurdles and strengths in social role functioning, in meeting economic and other basic needs, in family interactions, significant relationships and other social supports, and cultural factors. In order to reach an assessment, sources of data are the person, the family and significant others, the treatment team and records (Australian Association of Social Workers, 2015).

The findings of this study indicate that 66.2 percent of respondents are involved in the psychosocial assessment of patients. It is observed that except in the 41-50 years age group, almost an equal percentage of social workers in other age groups were involved in psychosocial study. The data indicates no difference in the percentage of respondents involved in the psychosocial study according to their sex. The study indicates that a substantial number of respondents in all educational categories are doing psychosocial studies.

Home Visits

Having an understanding of the psychological, social and physical aspects of the family life of the patient is necessary to plan the treatment efficiently. It is also crucial to collect adequate information so that our assessment has less chance of being based on hunches or prejudices, and this is obtained comfortably and successfully through home visits. At the WHO European Conference on Mental Hygiene Practice (1959), it was endorsed that home visits should be made with the intention of diagnosis as well as treatment and supervision of long-term patients in home care.

In a hospital setting, it is usually impossible for the physician to get an adequate view of the family background by interviewing the patient or family in the hospital. However, in a few minutes at home, an experienced observer can obtain more relevant information about the patient and his circumstances than during hours of exploring at the office. Home visits help a lot in appraising the problems of the patient and the relation of family interaction to these problems, personality features of the family members and studying the systems of intra-familial and interpersonal relations, knowing the socio-economic status of the family and the structure of interaction with the outer world.

The kith and kin of the patients have numerous wrong perceptions about many services, including medical and psychiatric treatment, mainly because of a lack of knowledge. The social worker can be convenient in educating the public about various illnesses and their treatment by making home visits and can pacify their illogical fears and eliminate misconceptions, etc. A pre-discharge home visit by the social worker improves the relations between the patients and their families are often drawn to the breaking point or it prevents further worsening of the relationship. The home visits also support preparing the family to receive the patients after discharge from the medical setting.

The data obtained from the study depicts that making home visits is not a frequent activity for male and female respondents in all age groups. Only 35.2 percent of respondents are making home visits. In all, 36.8 percent of respondents in the 20-30 years age group; 39.3 percent of respondents in the 31-40 years age group; 21.7 percent of respondents in the 41-50 years age group; and 34.8 percent of participants in 51 and above age group have visited homes of patients for assessment purposes. However, education-wise, respondents having an M.Phil. and Ph.D. degree are more involved in-home visits.

The following factors may be the probable reasons for the curtailment of home visits:

- Privacy: Patients are reluctant to give exact addresses, do not inform the change in address, do not want enquiries and refuse to disclose self-identity to the visitors.
- Confidentiality: Confidentiality is the major worry for the patients, particularly those having stigmatized diseases like STDs, HIV/AIDS, Leprosy, etc. They may be scared that confidentiality might be violated during home visits.
- Gender sensitivity: While doing home visits of female patients, the response of the spouses, family members and neighbors could be suspicious and give a reason for marital and family conflict.
- Logistic issues: Setting the most apt time for a home visit when the patient or the family is available at home can be a difficult task also. A lot of patients visiting hospitals are not residents of Delhi and come from different distant states and cities. Hence, home visits are not possible.

Referral

In Indian hospital settings, patients and their families come across certain issues or problems related to the treatment, such as the non-availability of beds due to problems with bed occupancy, non-availability of facilities for diagnostics and super specialty treatment, lack of financial resources to bear the expenses of treatment, accommodation problems during the course of treatment, rehabilitation in physical or mental disability, rehabilitation in unknown patients and so on. All these situations necessitate referral of patients to individuals (doctors and social workers) and organizations (hospitals/ treatment centers and community welfare agencies/NGOs). Hence, it is imperative for hospital social workers to know and utilize other persons and agencies just as the doctor knows and uses other professionals and technicians such as the dietician, the X-ray or lab technician, the nurse and the social worker. Here, the medical social worker is a bridge between the doctor, patient and resources available in the community.

Social workers refer the patients to different persons and organizations to facilitate their treatment or rehabilitation. Generally, the patients are referred to treatment centers, vocational training centers, residential institutions, charitable organizations, etc. The findings of the study describe that 63.4 percent of respondents referred patients to doctors, 57.2 percent of respondents referred patients to hospitals, 59.3 percent of respondents referred patients to social workers and 82.2 percent of respondents referred patients to other government and private organizations.

Public Relations

Public relation is one of the most important activities of hospital social workers. It includes meeting donors, meeting the medical team and mobilizing resources on behalf of patients. It is found that 48.3 percent of social workers are meeting donors; 65.5 percent of respondents regularly meet medical teams involved in the treatment of patients to know and apprise factors associated with the illness and remedy; and 68.3 percent of respondent are mobilizing resources to facilitate treatment for patients.

Administration

Administrative functions include many activities like maintaining a daily diary, documents and records, generating annual reports, preparing plans for projects, participating in budget formation, participating in hospital committees, doing internal and external correspondences and so on. In all, 66.2 percent of respondents in the study are engaged in administrative tasks. The study describes that respondents in all age groups are performing administrative tasks. It is observed that the percentage of respondents' involvement in administrative work is the highest in the 51 and above age group. In other age groups, there is not much difference seen. Gender-wise, 69.3 percent of females and 61.4 percent of males are doing administrative work. Respondents in all levels of education are also involved in administrative work, though the percentage is higher (80%) in M.Phil. and (100%) in Ph.D. respondents.

It is also observed that respondents are given only minor administrative responsibilities. They are not engaged in major administration-related activities like admissions, budget preparation, representation in hospital committees and policy making. Only 11 percent of respondents informed that they participate in preparing the annual budget of the department. About 33.8 percent of respondents said that they are consulted before making policy making or planning pertaining to their department. About 22.8 percent of respondents have representation in various committees.

Research/Data Collection

Trained social workers initiate, direct and participate in research-related activities with other social workers and healthcare team members on various topics such as social, economic and psychological aspects of illness/health, KAP studies, program evaluation studies, follow-up studies, explorative studies, comparative studies, interventional studies, etc. 64.8 percent respondents informed that they are involved in data collection/research related activities. The study reveals that the percentage of respondents involved in research and data collection is highest in the 20-30 years age group and lowest in the 41-50 years age group. This indicates that the younger generation is more interested in research-related work.

The data also indicates that almost an equal percentage of male and female respondents are involved in research and data collection activities. More than sixty percent of respondents from all educational backgrounds are participating in research activities. About (26.2%) of participants of the study informed that the results of their studies were implemented. The research studies of (18.6%) respondents were published. More than twenty percent of respondents independently conducted research activities.

Teaching, Training and Supervision

Modern hospitals not only offer clinical services but also run several academic programs via affiliated medical colleges and universities. Social workers, being integral parts of the healthcare team, are actively involved in teaching students of different disciplines like medicine, social work, public health, health education, nursing, occupational therapy, etc. They also provide orientation, training and supervisory service to social work students in field work, nursing students, interns and NSS volunteers. They closely liaison with social work departments in curriculum development by giving valuable inputs from the field so that social work education becomes relevant to the needs of people. Apart from this, hospital social workers are engaged in developing and organizing regular in-service training and continuing medical education of doctors, nurses, para-medical and administrative staff on various departmental/patient care activities and participate and organize conferences, seminars, symposiums for knowledge exchange and skill enhancement.

The findings of this study show that (49%) of respondents are supervising social work students, (23.4%) of respondents are teaching medical students, (24.8%) of respondents teach nursing students, and (8.3%) of respondents train and supervise students from other disciplines. The percentage of respondents involved in teaching all categories of students is greater in the 41 and above age group as compared to other age groups. A higher percentage of male participants are involved in teaching social work and medical students, whereas females are more into teaching nursing students. Participants with higher education (M.Phil. and Ph.D.) are more involved in teaching and supervising social work, medical and nursing students.

Table 2.1: Functions of Respondents

Function	Percentage of Respondents
Counseling	93.1%
Psychosocial Assessment	66.2%
Home Visit	35.2%
Referral	
Doctor	63.4%
Hospital	57.2%
Social Worker	59.3%
Others	82.2%
Meeting Medical Teams	65.5%
Resource Mobilization	68.3%
Administration	66.2%
Research/Data Collection	64.8%
Teaching & Supervision	
Social Work Students	49%
Medical Students	23.4%
Nursing Students	24.8%

The researcher also attempted to illicit information about the participation of hospital social workers in other academic pursuits. While 17.9 of the respondents informed that they are involved in organizing case conferences, 11 percent have participated in organizing symposiums, 35.9 percent of the respondents have assisted in organizing seminars and 22.8 percent of the participants have contributed to research activities of the department in previous two years.

Problems/Issues of Patients Addressed by Professional Social Workers

Economic Problems

In our country, a substantial proportion of the population lives under the poverty line. A greater number of people belong to the middle or lower middle strata. Often, patients falling in these categories face a shortage of finances to receive desired treatments and meet their healthcare needs. Such patients are referred to social workers who facilitate financial assistance through various funds available from the hospital, government and other private sources. Data reveals that 82.1 percent of hospital social workers deal with the economic or financial problems of the patients and facilitate the treatment of needy and indigent patients through the above-mentioned schemes of financial assistance. Apart from this, they are involved in the exemption of hospital charges as per the hospital policy. They also network and coordinate with NGOs and community welfare agencies to mobilize resources for the care of patients.

Housing/Accommodation

Delhi, as the capital and the central place of the country, is a hub of healthcare institutes (government and private) providing specialty, super specialty and referral services. Patients from across the country come here seeking treatment for numerous diseases and ailments. Many times, patients and their relatives need to stay there till the patients recover after the treatment. This necessitates the relocation of patients and their caregivers. Professional social workers in hospitals guide and refer patients to temporary shelters like dharmshala, vishram sadan, guest houses, etc. It is observed that 53.1 percent of the respondents used to handle housing or accommodation-related issues of the patients coming to different hospitals for treatment in Delhi.

Hospital Procedures

When the patients enter the hospital, they are not very aware of the hospital environment. They need to be acquainted with the facilities available in the hospital, like emergency, OPD and diagnostics, including the procedures and protocols involved in the treatment process. They (patients and families) require clear and precise information about the disease, its treatment options, investigations, medicines, regular follow-ups, etc. The study shows that 78.6 percent of the respondents are providing assistance to the patients and their attendants regarding hospital procedures involved in the treatment of patients.

Beliefs and Values

Few diseases have specific issues pertaining to the beliefs attached to the disease and societal attitudes towards patients suffering from them, like HIV, AIDS, Leprosy, Skin Diseases, Mental Illness, etc. The study indicates that 63.4 percent of the participants are also dealing with the beliefs and value systems of the patients in relation to their treatment in hospital settings.

Lack of Community Resources

Social workers working in public health facilities face the problem of limited resources available at the disposal of the hospital. On occasions, it becomes challenging to explain to the patients and their families why the required resources cannot be made available to all the clients and why they are referred to organizations outside the hospital. In the present study also, it is observed that 73.8 percent of hospital social workers are dealing with the problem of inadequate community resources to meet the healthcare needs of the patients.

Personality Problems

The findings of the study indicate that 60 percent of the respondents dealt with personality problems on the part of the patients.

Communication Problem

Carrying out purposeful communication includes knowing and eliminating difficulties in treatment, helping patients to accept illness and treatment, assisting in family's acceptance of the patient and enlisting their cooperation in the treatment. The researcher has analyzed the data of communication and language problems in dealing with patients by social workers in hospital settings. As per data, 59.3 percent of respondents revealed communication problems and 51 percent of the respondents had faced problems of understanding and communicating in the appropriate language. Social workers are among the frontline manpower of the hospital that help the patients and families to get the desired treatment. Hence, they are prone to face anger, which, at times, is the result of the dissatisfaction of patients and relatives in the course of treatment. It is found that 35.2 percent of the respondents receive threats from the patients or their attendants on certain occasions. At times, social workers are made to take up non-professional and multiple tasks by hospital authorities. In this study, 36.6 of the respondents also revealed that they face work pressure from the hospital authorities.

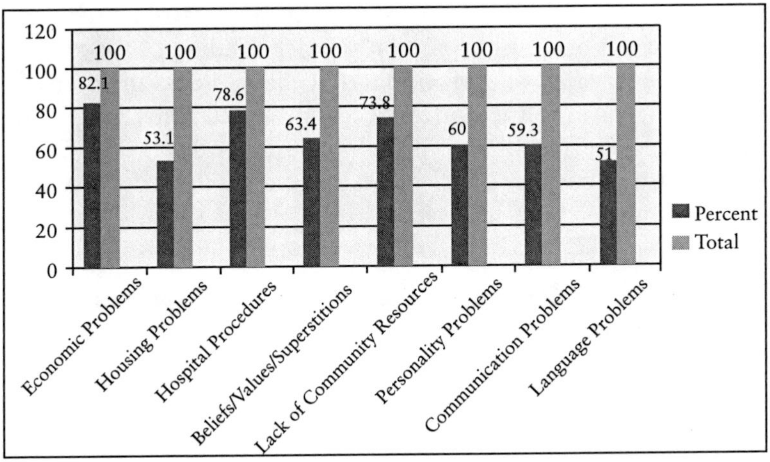

Graph 2.1: Problems Addressed by Respondents

Role of Hospital Social Workers

The use of the word "role" instead of more usual day-to-day words is only allowed if it keeps analytical possibilities, which they do not. The phrase 'seeing their role within the organization' may mean looking at their job, skill, profession and place in the total work situation; all of which are clearer in descriptive terms than the phrase used. The concept of role has severe theoretical limitations deriving from the lack of a general theoretical model of the social system and, more particularly, in this case, a clear definition of organization.

Role or role behavior means how the status occupant should act towards an individual or individuals with whom his status, rights and obligations put him in contact. Every person occupies positions or statuses within a number of status systems, and a status system may be perceived as a map that points out different statuses in conjunction to one another and shows how they are interrelated. A person's status is represented by his position on such a map.

The role is also defined as an individual's organized patterns of behaving, led by the status or functions he carries into one or more persons. The behavior pattern is opted, designed and colored by several dynamic factors such as the needs and motives of the person, the person's understanding of the mutual commitments and suppositions that have been invested by customs, traditions and conventions in the particular status and duties he performs, the compatibility or conflict between the person idea of responsibilities and presumptions and those held by others with whom he reciprocates.

'Role' has three components:

- Role Conception: An idea of how a person is required to perform in a given situation.
- Role Expectation: The way in which others generally expect from the occupant of a particular position to perform.
- Role Performance: The task performed by the individual.

Hospital social workers are involved in patient care at the case and organizational level. At the case level, social workers increase awareness of the multidisciplinary healthcare teams about a person's social situations and individual conditions by disclosing and explaining the relevant factors and subsequently enlarging the reality basis for medical assessment and treatment. At organizational level, social workers are involved in ensuring the optimum utilization of community services and supporting the patient in the readjustment to community life. Collaboration with agencies may facilitate gaining or escalating knowledge of the needs of particular groups of patients.

It is concluded that professional social workers in hospital settings perform multifaceted roles and activities. The majority of their work encompasses direct patient services like psychosocial evaluation, counseling, referrals, interaction with treating teams, meeting donors and mobilizing resources for the patients. Home visit, which is considered a primary tool of social work intervention, is practiced only at a miniscule level. In addition to this, they undertake administrative work, but their participation in vital administrative functions is very much restricted. They are also involved in teaching training supervision and research-related activities in a limited manner. While discharging their duties, medical social workers address an array of issues related to the care and treatment of patients and their caregivers and provide an important link to sort out these problems. The functions of hospital social workers, as enumerated in the chapter, suggest that they play multiple roles, such as counselor, educator, enabler, advisor, facilitator, broker, care-coordinator, trainer, researcher and consultant. They are powerful patient' advocates and a bridge between the patient, the doctor and organizations.

References

Albrithen, A., and Yalli, N. (2013). "A discussion of professional issues of hospital social workers in Saudi Arabia", *Social Work in Healthcare*, 52(1), 20-42.

Albrithen, A., and Yalli, N. (2015). "Hospital social workers in Saudi Arabia: Characteristics and functions", *Social Work in Healthcare,* 54(2), 158-76.

Beder, J. (2006). *Hospital social work: The interface of medicine and caring*. New York: Routledge, Taylor and Francis Group, U.S.A.

Bergman, A.S., Contro, N., Zivetz, N. (1984). "Clinical social work in a medical setting", *Social Work Health Care,* 9(3), 1-12.

Berkman, B. (1996). "The emerging health care world: Implications for social work practice and education", *Social Work*, 4(15), 511-52.

Bor, R., and Allen, J. (2007). "Counselling" in S. Ayers, A. Baum, C. McManus, S. Newman, K. Wallston, J. Weinman, R. West, (Eds.),

Cambridge Handbook of Psychology, Health and Medicine (2nd ed.). New York: Cambridge University Press.

Cowles, L.A., and Lefcowitz, M.J. (1992). "Interdisciplinary expectations of the medical social worker in the hospital setting", *Health and Social Work,* 17(1), 57-65.

Cowles, L.A., and Lefcowitz, M.J. (1995). "Interdisciplinary expectations of the medical social worker in the hospital setting": Part 2. *Health and Social Work,* 20(4), 279-86, https://doi.org/10.1093/hsw/20.4.279.

Craig, S.L., and Muskat, B. (2013). "Bouncers, brokers and glue: The self-described roles of social workers in urban hospitals", *Health and Social Work*, 38(1), 2013.

Cleak, H.M., and Turczynski, M. (2014). "Hospital Social Work in Australia: Emerging Trends or More of the Same?", *Social Work in Health Care*, 53, 199-213.

Coquillette, B.L., et al. (2015). "Social work services utilization by children with medical complexity", *Maternal and Child Health Journal*, 2015, 19, 2707-2713.

Davis, C., Baldry, E., Milosevic, B., and Walsh, A. (2004). "Defining the role of the hospital social worker in Australia", *International Social Work,* 47(3), 346-58.

Ferguson, S.S., et al. (2018). "Perceived workforce challenges among clinical social workers in hematopoietic cell transplantation programs", *Biology of Blood and Marrow Transplantation,* 24(5), 1063-68.

Fraher, E.P., Richmond, E.L., and Zerden, L.D.S. (2018). "Social work student and practitioner roles in integrated care settings", *American Journal of Preventive Medicine*, 54(6S3), S281-89.

Fudemberg et al. (2016). "Overcoming barriers to eye care: Patient response to a medical social worker in a glaucoma service", *Journal of Community Health*, 41, 845-49.

Greene, G.J., and Kulper, T.K. (1990). "Autonomy and professional activities of social workers in hospital and primary health settings", *Health and Social Work,* 15(1), 38.

Guo, K.L., and Company, J.D. (2007). "Leaders in hospital-based social work: The roles and functions of directors of social work in the case management model", *Leadership in Health Services,* 20(2), 124-33.

Hou, J.W., Hollenberg, J., and Charlson, M.E. (2001). "Can physicians' admission evaluation of patients' status help to identify patients requiring social work interventions?", *Social Work in Health Care,* 33(2), 17-29.

Judd, R.G., and Sheffield, S. (2010). "Hospital social work: Contemporary roles and professional activities", *Social Work in Health Care*, 49(9), 856-71.

Meyers, A., Bailly, C., Rheaume, S., Riley, K., and DeChillo, N. (2001). "A pilot survey of social work services in pediatric primary care programs in urban teaching hospitals", *Ambulatory Pediatrics,* 1(5), 259-61.

Muskat, B. et al. (2017). "Complex families, the social determinants of health and psychosocial interventions: Deconstruction of a day in the life of hospital social workers", *Social Work in Health Care*, https://doi.org/10.1080/00981389.2017.1339761

National Association of Social Workers. (2005). *NASW Standards for social work practice in health care settings.* Retrieved from http://www.socialworkers.org/practice/standards/naswhealthcarestandards.pdf.

Okoye, U.O. (2019). "Healthcare social work in Nigeria", in R. Winnett, R. Furman, D. Epps, and Lamphear, G. (Eds.). *Health Care Social Work: A Global Perspective* (pp. 149-61). New York: Oxford University Press.

Pockett, R. and Beddoe, L. (2017). "Social work in health care: An international perspective", *International Social Work,* 60(1), 126-39.

Sarah, G., Christina, A. and Browne, T. (2019). "Establishing the place of health social work", *Health and Social Work*, 44(2), 69-71.

Slana, M., et al. (2016). "Social work in hospitals in Slovakia: Current working conditions and difficulties in the view of the professionals", Sociologie si Asistenta Sociala-Tom IX/1, 81-89.

3

Profile and Status of Hospital Social Workers

In the present study, the data is collected from professional social workers employed by major hospitals in Delhi regarding their status through interview schedules. The first section of the interview schedule is concerned with the demographic characteristics of respondents. The other section is concerned with the service conditions, job satisfaction, problems and professional needs of social workers. The findings pertaining to the above-mentioned variables have been presented in such a way that the reader gets an overall view of the current situation of the medical social workers.

Age

Age is one of the most important biological characteristics of the individual and a vital factor in the analysis of the profile of the participants that cannot be overlooked. It determines the nature of the social category of people because it is one of the bases for the ascription of status and its relation to social organization. In the analysis of the profile of the respondents, age is an essential factor, mainly when we deal with such aspects as the participation of respondents in significant functions of the organization.

Table 3.1 analyses the respondents according to their age groups. The sample has been classified into four age groups ranging from twenty years and above. It is observed that among the 145 respondents, 26.2 percent are less than 30 years of age;

42.1 percent fell in the age group of 31-40 years; 15.9 percent are in the age group of 41-50 years; and the remaining 15.9 percent are above 51 years of age. It is concluded that the majority of social workers in the hospital setting under the study are quite young, and only 15.9 percent are seniors with more than 50 years of age.

Table 3.1: Age-wise Distribution of Respondents

Age (years)	Number of Respondents	Percentage
20-30	38	(26.2%)
31-40	61	(42.1%)
41-50	23	(15.9%)
51 and above	23	(15.9%)
Total	145	(100%)

Sex

Sex is another most apparent fact about any person and cannot be ignored while attempting data analysis of a scientific study. Like the teaching and nursing professions, medical social work is also regarded as a conventional female profession, which has evolved as an extension of the customary role functions of the females in the family in tasks requiring nurturing, socializing and helping. Women are supposed to play an expressive role in society that accentuates the value of emotions, spontaneous relationships, warmth and a humanistic approach. On the other hand, males are expected to undertake an instrumental function that is supposed to be logical, rational and productive. Services with patients involve a natural and humanistic approach. This does not mean that males cannot be uninhibited and humanistic, but the Indian culture gives importance to the male productive responsibility, and men are not supposed to be expressive as far as their emotions are concerned.

Table 3.2 presents the sex-wise distribution of the respondents under the present study. It is found that 60.7 percent of hospital social workers are female and 39.3 percent of hospital social workers are male. The data depicts that females are more oriented to opt for social work in medical settings than males.

Table 3.2: Sex-wise Distribution of Respondents

Sex	Number of Respondents	Percentage
Male	57	(39.3%)
Female	88	(60.7%)
Total	**145**	**(100%)**

Category

Manifested in Articles 15 and 16 of the Indian Constitution, the reservation system in India allows the government to set quotas in education and employment for certain socially disadvantaged groups like Scheduled Castes (SC), Scheduled Tribes (ST) and Other Backward Classes (OBC) to ensure their representation in public life.

Table 3.3: Category-wise Distribution of Respondents

Category	Number of Respondents	Percentage
General	109	(75.2%)
Other Backward Class	18	(12.4%)
Scheduled Caste	15	(10.3%)
Scheduled Tribe	03	(2.1%)
Total	**145**	**(100%)**

The study reveals that hospital authorities also gave representation to different categories while recruiting hospital social workers in Delhi. Table 3.3 shows that 75.2 percent of respondents in the study belong to the general category, 12.4 percent of respondents are OBC, 10.3 percent are SC and 2.1 percent are from the ST category.

Educational Qualifications

Education is an important component of demographic study as it is related to the standard of living and higher status of people in the community or society. It also indicates the level of technical knowledge and expertise of a person in their field of work. In our country, social work education mostly begins with a postgraduate degree in most of teaching institutions. Also, a postgraduate degree is widely accepted as a basic minimum qualification for the appointment of social workers in hospital settings.

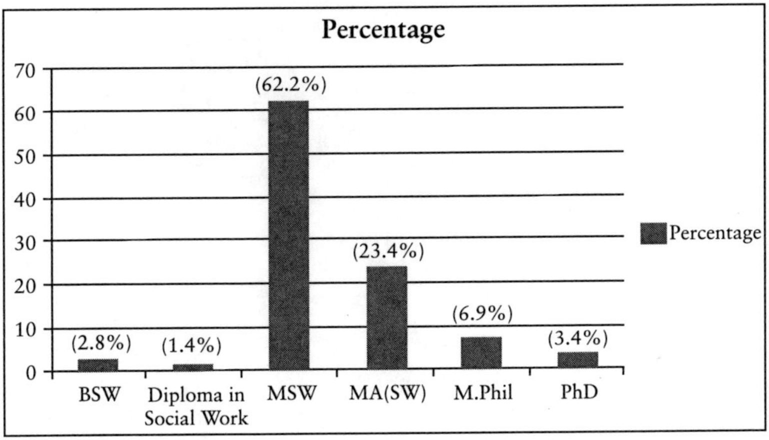

Graph 3.1: Education-wise Distribution of Respondents

The present study supports this fact. It reveals that 2.8 percent of the respondents have a bachelor's degree in social work, 1.4 percent hold a diploma in social work, 62.2 percent hold Master of Social Work (MSW) degree, 23.4 percent did Master of Arts (MA) in social work, 6.9 percent did M.Phil., and 3.4 percent of the respondents hold Ph.D. in Social Work/ Psychiatric Social Work qualifications. Hence, it is found that the majority of hospital social workers are postgraduate in social work.

Area of Specialization

In our country, a large number of social work institutions are imparting education and training in social work. Some institutes teach generic social work courses, and few others offer specialization courses at postgraduate level. The specialization in Medical and Psychiatric Social Work gives complete exposure to social work students about their roles and functions in hospital settings. Other specializations except HIV/AIDS, Family and Child Welfare and Generic Course do not provide any orientation in medical services and medical settings.

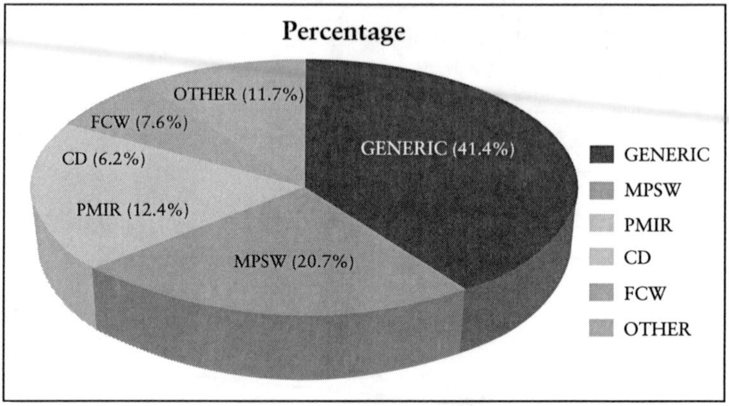

Graph 3.2: Specialization-wise Distribution of Respondents

It is observed in this study that 20.7 percent of the respondents have specialization in medical and psychiatric social work, 12.4 percent in personnel management and industrial relations, 6.2 percent in community development, 7.6 percent in family and child welfare and 11.7 in other specialization like correctional administration, HIV/AIDS, social policy, etc. The data also demonstrates that 41.4 percent of the respondents have studied generic courses in social work.

Type of Hospital

Although the government has framed guidelines for the appointment of a minimum number of social workers in hospitals and medical colleges, yet, its implementation depends upon the willingness of different hospital authorities to recruit hospital social workers. In practice, there are variations in the appointment of medical social workers. This study points out that the majority of hospital social workers in Delhi are employed in government hospitals, and private hospitals are not very keen on recruiting trained social workers. Even within the government sector, the central government-run hospitals and medical colleges appear to recognize the value of hospital social work more than the state government-run hospitals. As per the data, 65.5 percent of the respondents are employed in central government hospitals, 25.5 percent are working in hospitals which fall under the jurisdiction of state government and only 9.0 percent are employed by private hospitals.

Table 3.4: Distribution of Respondents by Type of Hospital

Type of Hospital	Number of Respondents	Percentage
Central Government	95	(65.5%)
State Government	37	(25.5%)
Private	13	(9%)
Total	**145**	**(100%)**

Length of Service

Length of service is an important determinant of one's contentment/adjustment in the current job. It also throws light on the trends of recruiting manpower in a particular section or department of the organization. The results of the study show that 40 percent of respondents have around five years of experience. About 22.8 percent of respondents have working experience in the range of ten years. Only 6.9 percent of respondents are working for twenty years and 18.6 percent of respondents are working for more than twenty years. It is observed that the majority of respondents in the study have five years of experience and are young. The findings of the study also indicate that a greater number of professional social workers have been employed in the last ten years in hospital settings in Delhi.

Table 3.5: Distribution of Respondents by Length of Service

Length of Service (years)	Number of Respondents	Percentage
0-5	58	(40%)
6-10	33	(22.8%)
11-15	17	(11%)
16-20	10	(6.9%)
21 and above	27	(18.6%)
Total	145	(100%)

Nature of Appointment

The type of appointment, i.e., permanent, temporary or contractual, is directly linked to the job security for the employee. While the regular or permanent employees feel more secure in the jobs, other temporary and contractual personnel may not enjoy security and satisfaction in their jobs. In the current study, it is observed that 51 percent of respondents are working in permanent positions; 4.1 percent are temporary and 44.8 percent are employed as contractual employees of major hospitals in Delhi.

Table 3.6: Distribution of Respondents by Nature of Appointment

Nature of Appointment	Number of Respondents	Percentage
Permanent	74	(51%)
Temporary	06	(4.1%)
Contractual	65	(44.8%)
Total	145	(100%)

Salary

The salary is yet another vital component of job satisfaction for the employee. The salary that is commensurate with the education and experience of the person not only increases their job satisfaction but also encourages them to perform better in the current job. On the other hand, less salary or discrepancies in salary structures result in dissatisfaction and a half-hearted approach to the work performance of an employee. It is observed that an equal percent of respondents (35.2%) draw a salary of up to ₹ 40,000 and ₹ 40,001-70,000, 13.1 percent are taking a salary in the range of ₹ 70,001-1 Lakh and 16.6 percent has their salary above ₹ 1 Lakh. It is also found that permanent employees are drawing higher salaries than contractual employees.

Table 3.7: Salary-wise Distribution of Respondents

Sr. No.	Range of Salary	Number of Respondents	Percentage
1	Up to 40000	51	(35.2%)
2	40001-70000	51	(35.2%)
3	70001-1 Lakh	19	(13%)
4	1 Lakh and above	24	(16.6%)
	Total	145	(100%)

Independent Room or Cabin

The job of a medical social worker requires personal contact with patients, interviewing, personal service and maintenance of records. Interviewing and counseling involve the disclosure of personal information and private matters. Privacy is vital, of course, because people are likely to be guarded in revealing personal information and expressing feelings if other people can see or hear them. Likewise, interviewers sometimes struggle to concentrate or express themselves when others can listen them. Because interviews sometimes involve intense emotional involvement by participants, freedom from distraction is a critical requirement. Telephone calls, knocks on the door and external noises can impair concentration and disrupt meaningful dialogue. Moreover, clients are unlikely to feel important and valued if social workers permit avoidable intrusions.

Having a desk between an interviewer and interviewee(s) emphasizes the authority of the social worker. For some clients, emphasizing the authority or position of the social worker may be a helpful way to indicate that they occupy a formal, appropriate position. All these necessitate a provision of a separate cabin for the social workers. The number of rooms or spaces allotted will, however, depend upon the size of the hospital and the expected load of work. Where there is a lack of space, it may be required to share a room with another department at the initial stage of establishment of the department, but a separate room is essential for conducting interviews in privacy. In a hospital where the in-patient and out-patient departments are close to each other, one department at the most convenient place would be sufficient, but if they are not so close to each other, one subordinate social worker may be provided either in the out-patient or in the in-patient department depending upon the load of work in the two situations. The social worker cannot interview the patients in a crowded place. A sense of privacy is essential during counseling if the patient is to bring out into the open those considerations which seem to him to be of particular importance. Hence, interview booths, both in the outdoor and indoor departments, should be provided. If they are in the same building, then each social worker should have one booth where s/he can interview both indoor and outdoor cases.

The medical social work department must be so located as to have easy access to telephone connections and clerical staff. The department, however small it might be, should be provided with a hospital attendant. It is desirable that every social worker should have an independent office room. If it is not possible to give a room to each social worker due to a shortage of space, then at least one big room with cubicles should be supplied to two or three social workers where each social worker can interview the clients in privacy. Equipment for the office should include tables, chairs, bookcases, filing cabinets, files for records, stationery, lamps and fans.

It is observed in the study that only 44.1 percent of respondents have independent room or cabin and 55.9 percent of respondents informed that they are sharing a room with other staff of the hospital. Male respondents (17.9%) and females (26.2%) respondents reported having independent room or cabin. In 31-40 years of age, (18.6%) respondents are given separate cabins. This is higher than other age groups. The percentage of respondents having an independent cabin is higher (26.9%) in central government hospitals than the other two types of hospitals. Around 22.8 percent of respondents in permanent positions and 19.3 percent in contractual positions have independent rooms or cabins.

Telephone Facility

A telephone facility is needed for communicating with the patients, their relatives, colleagues and other personnel working in the hospital and also with various organizations for referral, resource mobilization and rehabilitation of patients. 22.7 percent of males and 44.8 percent of females have telephone facilities. About (28.3%) of participants in 31-40 years were given telephone. In other age groups, a lesser percentage of respondents have phones. The majority of respondents (74.5%) are provided with a telephone facility. There is a higher percentage (49%) of respondents with telephone facilities in central government hospitals. About 42.1 percent of permanent and 29.7 percent of contractual social workers are provided with telephone facilities.

Computer Facility

Nowadays, hospitals have undergone computerization and digitalization. Therefore, this advanced technology has been commonly used by different professionals, including professional social workers. In the present study, it is found that 75.9 percent of respondents have computer facilities available to them. Among males (29.7%) and females (44.8%) have computers. In 20-30 years of age (18.6%); 31-40 years of age (28.3%); 41-50 years of age (14.5%) and above 50 years of age (13.1%), respondents are given computers. The percentage of respondents being provided with a computer is (39.3%) in permanent employees and (33.1%) in contractual social workers. About 51 percent of social workers in central government hospitals have computer facilities, which is higher as compared to social workers (17.2%) in state government hospitals.

Hospital Attendant

Hospital attendants are required to assist in day-to-day functioning of social workers. It is observed that only 56.6 percent of respondents are provided with hospital attendants, while the rest of the respondents used to do everything themselves without any assistance, which results in a waste of time for the social worker. While (20.7%) of males are provided with attendants; (35.9%) of females are given hospital attendants. Nearly the same proportion of respondents is given an attendant when they are between the ages of 20 and 40 and over 41.

Experience-wise, about 18.6 percent of respondents with five years of experience are provided with hospital attendants, which is more than in other higher-experience groups. About 35.9 percent of permanent social workers and 13.9 percent of contractual social workers have hospital attendants. The percentage (39.3%) of respondents given hospital attendants in central government hospitals is higher as compared to the percentage (11%) in state government hospitals.

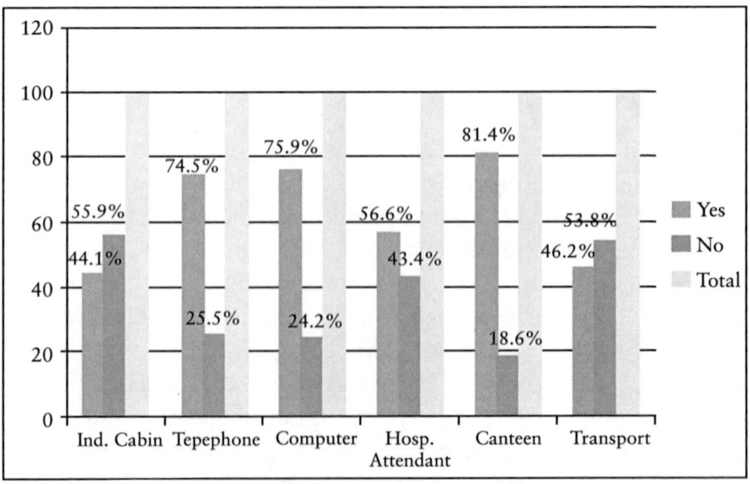

Graph 3.3: Distribution of Respondents in Work Facilities

Canteen Facility

Most of the hospitals in Delhi under the study are running canteen either on their own or outsourced. Hence the majority of social workers (81.4%) are benefiting from the canteen facility.

Transport Facility

The work profile of trained social workers in hospital settings comprises case studies, psychosocial evaluation and rehabilitation of patients for which they are required to visit their homes, schools, workplaces and community agencies. They are also conducting awareness generation activities in different organizations and communities on various healthcare issues. All these activities necessitate the availability of transportation facilities for social workers. If the transport facility is not provided by the hospital, it may lead to lots of waste of time and energy to travel with public transport.

It is observed in the study that only 46.2 percent of respondents are given transport facilities and 53.8 percent of respondents informed that they are working without any transport facility or allowance. About 32.4 percent of permanent and 11 percent of contractual respondents are offered transportation facilities. In central government hospitals, this percentage (35.9%) is higher than in state government hospitals. It is reported that hospital social workers who are employed in permanent service are enjoying more facilities than contractual social workers. This differentiation also exists between central government and state government hospitals.

Work Schedule

It is observed that 84.1 percent of hospital social workers are working in Day Shift, 9.7 percent of the respondents are working two shifts (Morning and Evening Shifts) and 6.2 percent of the respondents are working three shifts (Morning, Evening, and Night Shifts). 17.9 percent of the respondents informed that they remain on call and may be called upon to come to the hospital whenever required. Male respondents (32.4%) and (51.7%) females are doing general one shift. Age-wise, the highest percentage (37.2%) of respondents in 31-40 years of age is doing one shift duty. In the same age group, the highest percent of respondents remain on-call duty. Among respondents with 5 years of experience, (29.7%) are doing one shift; (7.6%) are doing two shifts; (2.8%) are doing three shifts duty and (7.6%) respondents remain on call. As the years of service increase, the percentage distribution of respondents in two shifts, three shifts and on-call duty fall down. It is concluded that junior-level social workers are mostly engaged in shift and on-call duties.

Workload

As regards the workload, 35.9 percent of the respondents reported a very heavy workload and 51 percent of the respondents informed that their workload is somewhat heavy. Only 7.6 percent of the participants viewed their workload as not heavy. The remaining 5.5 percent of the subjects could not describe how they perceived their workload. The data indicates that the majority of hospital social workers in all hospitals reported a somewhat heavy workload. A higher percentage of central government employees reported heavy workloads.

Job Supervision

The data depicts that the work of the majority of hospital social workers (65.5%) is supervised by medical professionals. Only 23.4 percent of social workers are supervised by senior social workers. In 2.1 percent of cases, administrative officer and other 9 percent of cases, respective departmental or unit in-charges are supervising their work. Findings reveal that the majority of the authority supervising the medical social workers is the personnel belonging to the medical profession, followed by the administrative officer. This concludes that the authority who supervises the work of Medical Social Workers belongs to a Non-Social Science background that may not be aware of the roles and functions of the medical social work practice. In most hospitals, a medical social worker functions as a single worker. Administratively, he is directly responsible to the head of the institution. If there are a number of medical social workers working in a hospital, they are attached to different departments like medicine, pediatrics, surgery, psychiatry, cardiac and so on. In our country, because of the early stage of development and since, in most cases, only one social worker is employed, the advantage of supervision by senior workers is almost absent.

Teamwork

Teamwork is important because professionals from different disciplines work towards the same goal of the treatment and care of the patients. Team practice is defined as that practice which is done by a group of people who possess individual expertise, who are responsible for making individual decisions within their disciplines, who hold a common purpose and who meet together to communicate, share and consolidate knowledge, from which plans are made, future decisions are influenced and actions are determined. Medicine has become highly specialized, and with specialization the concept of team practice has developed. Social workers, nurses, occupational therapists, physiotherapists, dieticians, psychologists and speech therapists are the members of the team in planning the treatment and rehabilitation of patients. Such a team should have scope for the exchange of views. In the study, 40.7 percent of the respondents informed that teamwork is greatly encouraged at their workplace; an equal percent of the respondents reported it to some extent and 15.2 percent of the respondents informed that teamwork is hardly encouraged at their workplace. Sex-wise, (15.2%) of males and (25.5%) of females informed that teamwork is greatly encouraged; (16.6%) of males and (27.6%) of females said that it is somewhat encouraged. Around 28 percent of young respondents opined that teamwork is encouraged to a great extent and about (30%) said that teamwork is somewhat encouraged. In central hospitals, a greater percentage of respondents believe that teamwork is highly encouraged.

Grievance Placement

Placing grievances in front of the authority is very important since it helps minimize the problems faced in jobs and increase job efficiency. But the way of placing it also matters a lot. Placing formally puts it into black and white form and becomes an official issue. Placing the grievances in an informal way shows the person's hopefulness for getting the solution without making it an official issue. Not placing the grievance shows that there is a lack of trust amongst the staff members towards the authority for getting justice, and this shows the indifferent attitude of the authority towards the welfare of the staff. So far as the grievance placement system is concerned, 24.8 percent of the respondents reported that they formally place their complaints, 20.7 percent of the respondents are doing it in informal ways, 42.8 of the respondents informed that they used to place their grievances in both formal and informal manner and 11.7 percent of the respondents stated that they do not place their grievances. Regarding formal ways, (11.7%) of males and (13.1%) of females register their complaints formally; (15.9%) of males and (26.9%) of females adopt both formal and informal ways to make complaints. In central hospitals, (15.9%) of respondents register their grievances formally; (26.9%) do it both ways; and (11%) informed that they do not make complaints. It is concluded that a majority of social workers mostly adopt both formal and informal manners of grievance placement.

Training and Continuing Education

In the study, 87.6 percent of hospital social workers informed that there are no refresher courses or continuing education in which they can participate from time to time. Only 32.4 percent of the respondents informed that they quite often participate in seminars/conferences/workshops pertaining to social work. About 54.5 percent of the respondents informed that there is no social work literature available in the library. It is seen that respondents having experience of up to ten years are participating more in conferences and workshops. With this, we can conclude that participation in conferences and seminars is very less amongst the medical social workers in hospitals in Delhi and needs to be increased.

Promotion

Promotion in a job helps to boost the spirit of work. Only 40 percent of respondents informed that there are opportunities for promotion to a higher grade in the current job. It is also observed that mostly (32.4%) avenues for promotion are available for central government employees. In state government and private hospitals, chances of promotion of hospital social workers to a higher position are negligible. Overall, it could be concluded that there are very less opportunities for promotion for Medical Social workers despite serving for so many years. This factor may hamper the job satisfaction level of Medical social workers.

Job Satisfaction

Job satisfaction describes how content an individual is with their job. It is concerning one's feelings or state-of-mind regarding the nature of their work. Job satisfaction is a relatively recent term since, in previous centuries, the jobs available to a particular person were often predetermined by the occupation of that person's parent. Job satisfaction can be influenced by a variety of factors, e.g., the quality of one's relationship with their supervisor, the quality of the physical environment in which they work, degree of fulfillment in their work, etc. The happier people are in their job, the more satisfied they are said to be. Job satisfaction is a very important attribute which is frequently measured by organizations. Job satisfaction has been defined as a pleasurable emotional state resulting from the appraisal of one's job, an affective reaction to one's job and an attitude towards one's job. This definition suggests that we form attitudes towards our jobs by taking into account our feelings, our beliefs and our behaviors. As Blum and Naylor quote in the book *Industrial Psychology: Its Theoretical and Social Foundations*, job satisfaction is the result of various factors. These factors are related to the job profile and are concerned with wages, steadiness of employment, conditions of work, advancement opportunity, recognition of ability, evaluation of work, social relations on the job, prompt settlement of grievances, fair treatment of the employer and other similar items.

Job satisfaction can be defined as a feeling of pleasure and contentment or the mental state of individuals regarding the nature of their work. A.M. Gesinde and G.O. Adejumo (2012) defined job satisfaction as "the gratification, happiness, compensation, fulfillment, joy, excitement, and self-actualization that individuals have from their jobs". According to Roopalekha, Melisha, and Latha (2011), "job satisfaction is a complex function of a number of variables. A person may be satisfied with one or more aspects of his or her job but at the same time may be unhappy with some aspects relating to it". Factors like physical conditions, salary and benefits, an opportunity for training and development, career progression and promotional avenues, reward system, the feeling of fulfillment in work, organizational policies and procedures, relationship with colleagues, supervision, grievance redress system, etc. influence the level of satisfaction among employees of an organization. Mohase and Khumalo (2014) says, "there is a connection between employee job satisfaction and patient satisfaction as healthcare workers who are dissatisfied with their job may have a poor attitude toward their job, be less productive, leave the job, or even have a negative effect on other staff". White (2000) states "satisfied employees tend to be more productive, creative, and committed to their employer". In this study, the researcher has presented the data pertaining to the extent of job satisfaction with multiple factors among hospital social workers in Delhi.

Satisfaction with Salary

Only 13.1 percent of the respondents stated that they are fully satisfied with the salary, 51 percent of the respondents are satisfied to some extent, and 35.9 percent of the respondents are not satisfied at all with the salary. In different ages, (2.8%) respondents within 50 years age group expressed full satisfaction with the salary. In thirty years age group, (11%) of respondents are somewhat satisfied and (12.8%) are not satisfied with the salary. Among forty years age participants, (22.8%) are somewhat satisfied and (16.6%) are not satisfied with their remunerations. The dissatisfaction with salary is higher in younger respondents within forty years of age. While (2.1%) of male respondents are fully satisfied with their salary, (22.1%) are somewhat satisfied and (14.8%) are not satisfied with the salary. Among female respondents, (10.3%) are completely satisfied, (29%) are somewhat satisfied, and (21.4%) are unsatisfied. Full satisfaction with salary is around (5.5%) among all junior and senior social workers. It is observed that dissatisfaction with salary is (13.8%) in respondents having 0-5 years of experience and (12.4%) with 6-10 years of experience, which is higher than other respondents having experience of more than ten years. The level of salary satisfaction improved with the length of service. The percentage of salary satisfaction is higher in employees of central government hospitals than in other hospitals.

Satisfaction with Work Facilities

Only 18.6 percent of respondents are fully satisfied with the work facilities being provided to them, 60.7 percent of respondents are satisfied to some extent and (20.7%) are not satisfied. The percentage of complete satisfaction is (6.9%) in the 31-40 age group respondents, and in other age groups, it is even lower. While (24.8%) respondents are somewhat satisfied in the same age group, (17.2%) are somewhat satisfied in the 20-30 age group. In other age groups, this satisfaction is lesser. Male respondents (7.6%) and females (11%) are fully satisfied with their salaries. About (23.5%) of males and (37.2%) of females are somewhat satisfied and (8.3%) of males and (12.4%) of females are not satisfied at all with their working environment. Satisfaction is higher in young social workers with ten years of experience. In central government hospitals, full satisfaction with the work environment is (7.6%), satisfaction to some extent is (37.9%) and dissatisfaction is (20%) which is more than in state government and private hospitals.

Satisfaction with Training Efforts

Only 16.6 percent of the respondents are fully satisfied with opportunities for training and continuing education given to the hospital's social workers; 35.9 percent of the respondents are satisfied to some extent and 47.6 percent of the respondents are not satisfied with the training efforts and opportunities in their hospitals. Among the 20-30 years age group (6.9%) of respondents are fully satisfied with training efforts, (8.3%) are somewhat satisfied and (11%) are not satisfied. Of respondents within 31-40 years of age (7.6%) are satisfied, (11.7%) are somewhat satisfied and (22.8%) are unsatisfied; in the 41-50 year age group, none of the respondents expressed full satisfaction with training efforts, however (7.6%) respondents are somewhat satisfied and (8.3%) are not satisfied at all. Other senior (2.1%) respondents are satisfied, (8.3%) are somewhat satisfied and (5.5%) are dissatisfied with training opportunities for hospital social workers. Full satisfaction with training efforts on the part of hospitals is slightly higher in respondents having five years of experience. The extent of satisfaction and dissatisfaction was higher in central government hospitals.

Satisfaction with Colleagues

As far as the relationship with other colleagues at the workplace is concerned, 52.4 percent of the respondents are fully satisfied, 46.9 percent of the respondents are somewhat satisfied and 0.7 percent of the respondents are not satisfied. Male respondents (24.1%) are fully satisfied and (14.5%) are somewhat satisfied with their colleagues. Among female respondents (28.3%) are satisfied and (32.4%) are partially satisfied. None of the female respondents is dissatisfied with their colleagues. Age-wise (22.1%) of respondents in the 31-40 years group expressed complete satisfaction and (20%) expressed somewhat satisfaction which is higher in all age groups. Apart from 20-30 years respondents (0.7%), no one said that they are dissatisfied with colleagues. Experience-wise, there was not much difference in satisfaction with colleagues. Among central hospital employees, the satisfaction level is higher as an equal percent (32.4%) of respondents informed their full and somewhat satisfaction with colleagues. In state govt. and private hospitals, no one showed dissatisfaction with colleagues.

Satisfaction with Healthcare Team

In the interaction between the social workers and healthcare teams, 40.7 percent of the respondents are fully satisfied, 50.3 percent of the respondents are somewhat satisfied and 9 percent of the respondents are not satisfied. Among the 20-30 years age group (9.7%) of respondents are fully satisfied, (12.4%) are somewhat satisfied and (4.1%) are not satisfied. Of respondents between 31-40 year's age (17.9%) are satisfied, (19.3%) are somewhat satisfied and (4.8%) are unsatisfied. In the 41-50 year age group, (5.5%) of the respondents expressed full satisfaction with the healthcare team; however, (4.3%) of respondents are somewhat satisfied and no respondent informed dissatisfaction. Other senior (7.6%) respondents are satisfied, (8.3%) are somewhat satisfied and no one is dissatisfied with the healthcare personnel. Satisfaction with the healthcare team is slightly higher among young social workers and central government employees.

Satisfaction in Meeting Patients' Needs

As regarding responding to the needs of patients and their families, 55.2 percent of the respondents are fully satisfied; 42.1 percent of the respondents are somewhat satisfied and 2.8 percent of the respondents are not satisfied at all. In meeting patients' needs (20.7%) of male and (34.5%) of females are fully satisfied; (17.9%) of males and (24.1%) of females are somewhat satisfied; and (0.7%) of males and (2.1%) of females are not satisfied. In the 31-40 year age group (26.9%) of respondents are absolutely satisfied in meeting the needs of patients, which is highest among all age groups. Almost equal percent of respondents in 20-30 and 31-40 ages are satisfied to some extent. Only in the 20-30 year age group (2.8%) of respondents showed dissatisfaction. In central government employees, the percentage of satisfaction in meeting patients' needs is higher than in other hospitals.

Overall Job Satisfaction

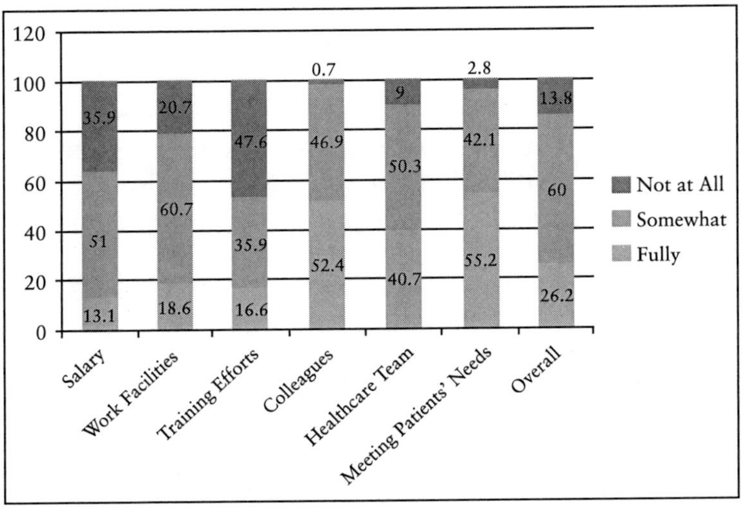

Graph 3.4: Extent of Job Satisfaction

In overall job satisfaction, about 26.2 percent of the respondents in the study indicated their full satisfaction in their current job; 60 percent of the respondents are satisfied to some extent only and the remaining 13.8 percent of the respondents said that they are not satisfied with their present job. Overall satisfaction is lower when analyzed according to gender, age and type of hospital.

Among males (8.3%) of respondents are completely satisfied, (24.8%) are partially satisfied and (6.2%) are unsatisfied with their job. Female respondents (17.9%) are fully satisfied, (35.2%) are somewhat satisfied and (4.6%) are dissatisfied with the job. Within thirty years (5.5%) of respondents are fully satisfied, (15.9%) are partially satisfied and (4.8%) are unsatisfied. In the 31-40 year age group (9.7%) of respondents are completely satisfied, (26.9%) are somewhat satisfied and (5.5%) are not satisfied. Among 41-50 aged respondents, (3.4%) are satisfied, (10.3%) are somewhat satisfied and (2.1%) are unsatisfied. Other senior respondents (7.6%) are fully satisfied, (6.9%) are partially satisfied and (1.4%) are not satisfied. In central hospitals (17.9%) of respondents are satisfied, (38.6%) are somewhat satisfied and (9%) are dissatisfied with the job.

The demographic characteristics of the respondents reveal that the majority of participants of the study are female and younger generation. Three-fourth of the respondents belong to the general category. The majority of respondents possess Master's level qualifications in social work. Hospitals didn't give any consideration to the specialization of the candidates in recruitment as only 20.7 percent of respondents in the study underwent specialized training in medical and psychiatric social work and 41.4 percent of respondents studied a generic course in social work. Central government hospitals are at the forefront of recruiting professional social workers. In all, 40 percent of respondents have five years' experience, which indicates that a greater number of social workers have been employed recently. An almost equal number of respondents is permanent and contractual. However, permanent employees are drawing higher salaries than contractual employees.

It is concluded that less than half of the respondents are provided independent rooms or cabins. About three-fourth of the respondents have the facility of telephone, computer and canteen; more than half of hospital social workers have hospital attendants for assistance in day-to-day work; and less than half of the respondents are provided with transportation as and when required. The majority of the respondents have five years of experience. More than three-fourth of the respondents are working in one general shift and others are doing shift duties. Nearly one-fifth of hospital social workers remain in on-call duty. Less than one-third of the respondents draw a salary in the range of rupees one lakh and above. Over three-fourth of the respondents reported a heavy workload. Less than one-fourth hospital social workers' work is supervised by senior social workers. Though teamwork is an essential element in hospital work yet, only about one-third of respondents informed that teamwork is greatly encouraged in hospitals. The majority of respondents adopt formal and informal ways to place their grievances. More than three-fourth of respondents informed that there is no continuing education/training/refresher course for hospital social workers. The majority of respondents do not participate in conferences, seminars and workshops, and hospitals and libraries also do not have social workbooks and journals. There are no opportunities for promotion for more than half of the respondents. In most hospitals, there is no association or union of social workers. Overall, only one-fourth of respondents are fully satisfied with their job.

References

Gesinde, A.M., and Adejumo, G.O. (2012). "Job satisfaction status of primary school teachers in Ota", Nigeria. *European Journal of Educational Studies*, 4(1), 11-18.

Jathanna, R., Melisha, R.D., Mary, G., and Latha, K.S. (2011). "Determinants of job satisfaction among healthcare workers at a tertiary care hospital", *Online Journal of Health and Allied Sciences*, 10(3).

Mohase, N., and Khumalo, J. (2014). "Job satisfaction in the healthcare services in South Africa: Case of MPH", *Mediterranean Journal of Social Sciences*, 5(3), 94-102, https://doi.org/10.5901/mjss.2014.v5n3p94

White, A.V. (2000). "Job satisfaction and professional development of health information administration faculty", *Allied Health*, 29(3), 129-37.

4

Conventional Social Work in Hospital Settings

The social work curriculum prescribes six methods of social work practice, i.e., case work, group work, community organization, social work research, social welfare administration and social action. Practice and theory are more advanced in social case work, but the other methods are advancing rapidly. Although case work has been predominantly used in healthcare settings, yet, group work, community organization and other methods are also entering and proving significant in healthcare. However, their application is uneven. This chapter describes what conventional methods of social work are applied by medico-social workers in exercising their duties in hospitals.

Social Case Work

Case work is a method to study, assess and treat individual and family problems based on knowledge of human behavior. Case work services entail not only working with individuals but also interactions with the family and other persons in organizations aimed at providing service to the client. Case work became dominant in medical social work in the forties. The official statements of standards for hospital social service departments, Chicago (1949) said that case work is the basic and major activity of the department and many more functions of the department rely on thoughtful and constant case work practice.

The psychosocial assessment in medical social case work is related to a person in a social situation that has relevance to the client's health outcomes. A range of elements relating to the person himself, his social functioning, social circumstances and the physical problem must be examined. This evaluation aims to decide the treatment goals and the emphasis of treatment. Nothing limits the medical social worker in determining if to work with the individual, the family or other significant ones. The MSW is free to work with one or all.

In social case work, a trained social worker provides professional assistance to the clients and their families on one-to-one basis to find solutions for their psychosocial problems and achieve better adjustment to their social conditions satisfyingly. Hollis (1954) defined case work as a technique used by social workers to assist persons in solving issues of social adjustment which the client is not able to do satisfactorily with his/her own endeavors. At times, due to certain external or internal factors, a client may have difficulties in adjusting to their social environment and/or availing of civic and developmental services and opportunities. In such a situation, the case worker helps the client to adjust to the situation or produce necessary alterations in the social system.

Perlman (1957) has discussed the dynamic components which make up the case work situation, namely, the person, problem, place, worker/professional and process. It means a person with a problem approaches the agency where the professional social worker helps him/her through systematic social case work. Richmond (1992) puts forward that it comprises the processes that evolve personality through adjustments purposefully impacted, person by person, between people and their circumstances.

An individual comes across a problem, which can either be physical, economic, psychological or relational and may arise out of some need or hindrance or acquisition of frustrations or maladjustments. The person is unable to resolve the problem on their own, which further disrupts their social functioning. In the process of social case work, a series of activities are facilitated to help the client make effective use of their strengths and the resources available in the community, thereby enabling a person to achieve better social functioning.

In hospital settings, a professional social worker functions as a member of the team comprising various healthcare professionals, and his work primarily revolves around interacting with the patients and their families regarding healthcare issues. Here, social case work techniques are utilized with the patients who are coming to OPDs, special clinics, emergency or admitted in ICUs and wards. For example, in mental healthcare or treatment of psychiatric illness, the case worker maintains rapport with the family members to interpret the needs of mentally ill patients and acts as a bridge between the doctors, the patient/family and the society in the treatment, follow-up and after care of such patients. Similarly, while working with chronically and terminally ill patients like patients suffering from heart disease, diabetes, HIV/AIDS, cancer, organ failure, etc., hospital social worker makes use of the case work method in providing guidance and psychosocial support to the patient and the family in apprising the illness, treatment protocols, adjustment with lifestyle and also ease out the financial burden for needy patients by mobilizing resources available at the hospital and community level.

The impetus in case work in the hospital setting is on the social aspects of the client's ailment, remedy and rehabilitation. Hospital social workers render services to those patients whose social condition causes the illness or hampers the treatment. In a few instances, he may interact with the patients of a specific group of diseases, where potential social problems are likely to play a role. For example, the social workers may meet every patient visiting a tuberculosis clinic, oncology unit or STD clinic. Thus, the stress in case work is on the medical and social problems of a patient. Medical social problem prevails when the medical aspect in a case situation influences the social, or the social aspect influences the medical or both (Pathak, 1961).

In Western countries, the patient requiring admission to a hospital first introduces themselves to the social worker. They interview the patient, gather all social history and place them in the classified group based on the ability to afford the treatment. This information is supplied to the admission staff that, after physical examination, sends the patient to the concerned ward.

In case the patient has not been interviewed by MSW; he may be referred to the social service Department. On the other hand, if the patient is critically ill or there is minimal doubt about eligibility, the patient may be admitted and interviewed later. After the routine social information such as age, sex, mental status, occupation and medico-social issues are ascertained, the patient is assigned to a medical social worker for more detailed information if required. The latter then deals with the client as long as mandatory. They make a thorough study of all relevant factors via personal interviews, home visits, visits to the employer, teachers and neighbors and community welfare organizations as needed.

The Indian scenario is completely different. After an OPD card is issued to the patient, s/he is provided consultation by the doctor, who may prescribe drugs and certain diagnostic procedures or suggest for admission. In the latter case, he is sent to the admitting staff. He may also refer the case to another hospital or put him on the waitlist. The hospital social worker is generally involved in clerical help for OPD cases or, at best, in reporting on his social and emotional factors to the physician. In certain hospitals, the patient is referred to the social service unit either by the OPD physician or the ward doctor. In a few cases, it is the social worker who goes to the patients. In many cases, patients are unaware of the hospital's social services and that they need this service. Hence, the case work process, many times, begins with an explanation to the patient of his/her need for this service in the treatment of the ailment.

In the present study, the researcher ascertained from the respondents the application of the social case work method in their practice as hospital social workers. In all, 81.4 percent of social workers informed that they are making use of social case work techniques in their practice. The percentage of respondents making use of social case work is highest (87%) in the 51 and above age group. A substantial percent of respondents in all age groups practice social case work. Sex-wise, the percentage is higher (85.2%) in females. At all education levels, the majority of hospital social workers practice social case work.

Social Group Work

Illness is not merely a personal issue. The patient is affected by the medical situation as a member of a social network, which in turn influences the nature of recovery. Therefore, illness cannot be treated in isolation. In the Indian social system, people live in very close-knit family. Culturally, the emphasis is on family and not on the individual. There is tremendous scope to use the methods of group work in helping sick and disabled people.

Applying group work techniques, the medical social worker enables the patients with corresponding problems to associate with others so that they feel less obscure and segregated. This could bring about a sense of affiliation and being a member of the community, which would encourage them to accommodate the larger community. Medical social workers can use this group as a therapeutic unit for emotional development and attitudinal modifications among the group members. Hence, the group can be used as a main instrument for mutual sharing and assistance. Multiple group activities for recreation, education and skill training of the patient and their relatives can be conducted.

In recent years, social workers initiated finding the possibility of using group work in medical settings. The application of the group work method has been acknowledged, and its utility is slowly increasing. The type of groups could be children in wards, patients with chronic disease, disabled patients requiring rehabilitation, etc. Group members discuss their feelings about illness and impairment, the hospital and its staff, their own use of medical care and rehabilitation, their behavior toward them and so on. At times, games, plays and music are used. Occasionally, the sessions are completely focused on group therapy.

Social group work is a method in which people in groups, a social agency or a community are assisted by a trained worker who guides their interaction in program activities so that they may associate themselves with others and experience growth opportunities according to their needs and capabilities towards personal, group and community development (Trecker, 1955). According to Murphy (1959) social group work is a technique that supports individuals to improve social functioning through purposeful group interactions and adjust to their individual, group or community issues.

Group work supports patients and families differently than case work. Members of a group assist one another in handling their problems while offering mutual concern. This method is specifically relevant at certain stages of life, like adolescence, when young people go out of the family and take their peers as ideals. While analyzing group work, Konopka (1983) presented a processed narrative of a series of seven meetings held by a group worker with a group of epileptic patients in their late teens and early twenties. She showed clearly how they were empowered through the group process to work with greater security in employment and other roles, as well as in day-to-day social life. In her evaluation, she described how the group process benefited in helping individuals. She analyzed group interaction, group discussion and reality testing to help agents. The role of the group worker was to provide support, information, help in gaining insight and referral to community agencies.

Social workers in hospital settings may extend group work by forming different kinds of groups like psycho-educational groups, patients' support groups, therapeutic groups, recreational groups, self-help groups, advocacy groups and single-session groups. Groups can be formed to solve problems at hand or provide counseling to members undergoing similar negative experiences. The main aim of group work practice is to give an opportunity for patients with similar ailments not to feel isolated, come together and develop belonging to resolve the problem and overcome other associated issues like anxiety, depression and adherence to treatment through mutual acceptance. Thus, the group is utilized as a therapeutic agent for bringing change in the attitude and emotional well-being of patients. Different group activities for recreation, education and skill development may be conducted. The group work method is widely used with patients suffering from HIV/AIDS, cancer, mental illness, alcoholism, drug abuse, physical disability, organ transplantation and so on.

Group work provides direct service to patients by forming natural groups in hospital wards, recreation rooms, etc., where patients generally assemble. Medical and long-stay facilities offer chances for such activities due to greater stability and continuity of patient groups. Group work theory emphasizes acknowledging the hospital as a social system, in which personnel hope for certain behavior patterns of patients, and patients, in their turn, arrive at their own understanding of the hospital and the staff. These patient attitudes can be equated with the inmate culture in the correctional institution. As would be expected, the combined use of case work and group work techniques has been found to be beneficial to several patients, as well as vitalizing to social workers (Ohlin and Lawrence 1959). Though the individual patient remains the centre of attention of the hospital social worker, yet, there is an obvious tendency found towards working with groups of patients and their families to reach a larger section of the population at once and tap the innate power of a group in the exercise of facing individual problems (Warde, 1987).

In the present study, it is found that 52.4 percent of social workers are using social group work methods in dealing with patients' health-related issues. A higher percentage (60.7%) of social workers in the 31-40 age group use group work techniques. There is not much difference in group work practice between males and females. All Diploma and Ph.D. respondents, 80 percent of M.Phil. respondents and 52.2 percent of MSW respondents are practicing group work in hospital settings.

Community Organization

Sieder (1959) defined Community Organization as a method of social work practice that assists a community to decide and accomplish continually more preferable program goals that meet regularly altering social welfare requirements by encouraging the interaction of its components (organizations, institutions, individual leaders and geographical subdivisions) in such a way as to make best use of its internal and external resources while at the same time building its potentials to solve new and tough issues. Its target is to help individuals and groups enhance their capabilities and urge them to work together to achieve progressive change and better amalgamation in the social services of the community. This is obtained by helping the community to identify needs, order these needs, make a plan to fulfill them, execute the action plan and analyze this action in terms of its sufficiency and outcomes.

The healthcare approach of developing countries has altered in recent years. The focus is no more on the individual only but on the community, too. With the inception of community health, the whole community is taken into consideration while program planning for preventive, curative and rehabilitation services. Therefore, a community diagnosis is made and treatment is provided at individual, family and community levels, in which the staffs from medicine and public health operate as a team. Because of the new concept of community medicine, the scope for medical social work intervention has significantly expanded. Now, the social worker is not only engaged in the treatment of the individual patient in the hospital but in many other health-related projects outside the hospital. His activities can be counted as follows:

- make community contacts undertake community surveys and explain the importance of the hospital to the community;
- gain knowledge of the community culture, health habits and practice trends and assist the medical team in knowing these practices and merging their positive aspects into the health services;
- enable the community to know the features of total health and how to promote it;
- make home visits to convince people about the value of preventive care and interpret the nature of the ailment and the treatment involved, thus diminishing any pathological effect;
- sensitize people regarding the right to health and encourage their participation and involvement in healthcare programs;

- plan skill-development or recreational programs on the basis of the felt needs of the people for educating them on several aspects of health and illness;
- establish new services with the help of the local leaders;
- formulate training programs for health workers belonging to the community to guarantee maximum participation and cooperation;
- coordinate with the government, civic bodies and different departments such as agriculture, housing, water supply and so on;
- work with community leaders and assist the policymakers to acknowledge the community needs so as to improve the total health of the people;
- organize educational and therapeutic activities and use them as modalities to create awareness and confidence in the public to manage their health; and
- work with individuals and families in need of help.

It is observed in the study that community organization as a primary method of social work is not practiced much by hospital social workers in Delhi. The data reveals that 33.1 percent of hospital social workers are involved in a community organization to educate people on various health-related problems and their treatment. An equal percentage (33%) of males and females use community organizations. Respondents with higher education (Ph.D. and M.Phil.) are using this method more than other respondents.

Social Action

Richmond (1922) first time defined social action as "mass betterment through propaganda and social legislation". This definition stresses improving the condition of a huge section of the population as an aim of social action, with propaganda and social legislation as the main strategy. The term social action is applied to that aspect of organized social welfare activity directed towards shaping, modifying or maintaining the social institution and policies that collectively constitute the social environment. According to Friedlander (1977), social action is an individual, group or community effort within the framework of social work philosophy and practice that aims to achieve social progress, modify social policies and improve social legislation and health and welfare services.

Social action is viewed as a "process of social work mainly concerned with securing legislation to meet mass problems". It is also defined social action as efforts to bring about change or prevent change in current social practices or situations through education, propaganda, persuasion or pressure on behalf of objectives believed by the social actionists to be socially desirable. Baldwin (1966) defined social action as an "organized effort to change social and economic institutions as distinguished from social work or social service, the fields of which do not characteristically cover the essential changes in established institutions. Social action covers movements of political reform, industrial democracy, social legislation, racial and social justice, religious freedom and civil liberty, its techniques includes propaganda, research and lobbying".

Social action, as a method of professional social work practice, is an organized effort to change or improve social and economic institutions through the organization and mobilization of the community people. Unlike other social work methods, social action emphasizes long-term essential changes in established social institutions. Social action covers movements of social, religious and political reform, social legislation, racial and social justice, human rights, freedom and civic liberty.

The social action process, more or less, passes through the recognizable and systematic stages. First of all, a scientific analysis or research on the social problems affecting the community people is carried out. Then, awareness is generated regarding various aspects of the problem, and people are encouraged to take collective and collaborative action to solve the problem. The third stage is centered on organizing people for coordinated and directed intervention, whereas in the further stage, suitable strategies are developed to achieve the goals, and lastly, action is taken. Every social action process passes through these stages, and professional social workers or actionists are well-equipped with the knowledge and skills required in different stages.

As a method of social work, social action adheres to the philosophy of professional social work. It does not blame people for the deficiency or problem. It strongly believes in the worth and dignity of human beings. Social action rejects the doctrine of laissez-faire and survival of the fittest. The unfit person has the same fundamental rights as the more fit. The rich and powerful are not necessarily fit, and neither the poor nor the weak are inherently unfit. It adopts a commitment to the capacity of all the people to take action to improve their life circumstances. It grounds this action on a process of open participation in which people, preferably collectively; explore the underlying social issues of their life situations as the foundation for action.

Practitioners do not lead, but through a non-elitist, highly skilled process, they facilitate members in making choices and taking action for themselves. Social Action involves a large number of people fighting for a particular cause. For example, social workers can raise their voices on behalf of the people living with HIV/AIDS.

The findings of the study indicate that social action is the least used traditional social work method by hospital social workers. Only 29.7 percent of the respondents informed that they were using social action to facilitate the treatment of patients coming to the hospital in Delhi. Younger social workers are practicing it more than senior social workers. More male respondents (38.6%) and more respondents at higher education levels look interested in using social action in their practice.

Social/Social Work Research

People-centered research is an overlooked area in healthcare system in India. A large number of social researchers are keen on cause-effect and cost-benefit analysis, whereas the need of the hour is inter-disciplinary research that looks into the varied social, psychological, economic and cultural aspects of the health of people. Hence, the "people" are kept backwards while the 'disease' and 'medicine' take the front seat in policy making. Social work research has the prospect to think of "people-centered" research in health, and the social worker has a vital role in enhancing social work research so as to support healthcare planning in the country. Hospital Social Workers could undertake research at different levels as follows:

- Independent Study: Medical social workers are trained in social research methodology and preparing dissertations in their course work; hence, they can independently undertake research projects on social, psychological, financial and rehabilitative aspects of patient's problems.
- Collaborative Projects: Social workers may collaborate with the physician in medico-social research such as on problems of peptic ulcer, cardiac patients, allergic patients, mental illness, attempted suicide, accidents, STDs/HIV/AIDS, etc.
- Clinical Research: Social workers are capable of carrying out sociological research and helping the physician in the inclusion of volunteers and analysis of the effectiveness of new vaccines, drugs or contraceptives. They may work as assistants or field workers in the research unit of a hospital.

To undertake research projects and guide research scholars, either independently or jointly with co-related disciplines, forms one of the crucial areas of tasks performed by hospital social workers. Recently, the involvement of social workers in multidisciplinary health research has been acknowledged as a formal activity. In the past, physicians used to invite social workers who were associated with them to participate in certain kinds of clinical research projects. Some of the findings were published in medical journals. With growing interest in psychosocial aspects of illness and the availability of funds for multidisciplinary research, projects are being formulated in which there is continual provision for a social worker on the project staff, and social workers are given chances to take part in the planning from the very inception.

The findings of this study show that 51.7 percent of social workers in hospitals are involved in social/social work research in their practice. Age-wise, the younger generation is more engaged in research/data collection. More male respondents seem enthusiastic about research activity. It is observed that although the percentage of respondents applying the social research method is higher among Ph.D. and M.Phil. degree holders, yet, overall a reasonable percentage of social workers in hospitals are using this method in their practice.

Social Welfare Administration

Social welfare is a broad system of agencies and programs which meets the welfare needs of society and within which social work operates (Bartlett, 1961). Administration may be considered as a set of procedures to link those who control the means for some tasks with those who use the goods or services produced by these means, e.g., pupils, patients, tenants and customers. Social welfare administration requires the administrator, who has to keep and develop collaboration among (i) the resource providers, (ii) the task performers who convert means into goods and services, and (iii) the users. If these three groups are not efficiently and regularly linked, the work cannot be done, and the concerned organization will, sooner or later, fail.

Hospital social workers normally function within a departmental structure with a director who holds complete responsibility for clinical and administrative supervision, formulation and implementation of policies and protocols, data management, record maintenance, finance, recruitment, deputation and discipline of staff. Directors also form practice guidelines and make sure that standard protocols are followed. They offer opportunities for in-service education to maintain a knowledge base of current issues, make programs, and warrant that staff credentials are up to date.

Table 4.1: Application of Conventional Social Work Methods

Social Work Method	Percentage of Respondents
Social Case Work	81.4%
Social Group Work	52.4%
Community Organization	33.1%
Social Action	29.7%
Social Work Research	51.7%
Social Welfare Administration	52.4%

Administration involves clerical activities like keeping records, registers, etc.; planning and conducting day-to-day activities of the department; supervising and consulting the staff and volunteers; and liaison with hospital authorities so as to keep them updated and engaged in the planning and implementation of departmental programs for patient care and the staff development. Data obtained from the study indicates that 52.4 percent of the respondents are using the Method of Social Welfare Administration to help needy patients to access healthcare. Age-wise, the percentage of senior social workers (65.2%) using this method is higher than in other age groups. More males (56.1%) appear to practice social welfare administration. At all educational levels, social workers are using this method; however, the percentage is higher (80%) in Ph.D. degree holders.

On the basis of the data, it is concluded that more than three-fourth of hospital social workers use techniques of social case work and over half of the respondents use social group work, social research and social welfare administration. Community organization and social action are the least practiced methods by hospital social workers. Hence, it may be concluded that social case work is being used by the majority of social workers in Delhi, and other methods of social work practice are not being applied at the optimum level.

References

Bartlett, H.M. (1961). *Social Work Practice in the Health Field.* New York: National Association of Social Workers.

Friedlander, W.A. (1977). *Introduction to Social Welfare.* New Delhi: Prentice Hall.

Hollis, F. (1964). *Casework: A Psychosocial Therapy.* New York: Random House.

Konopka, G. (1983). *Social Group Work: A Helping Process* (pp. 125-79). New Jersey: Prentice-Hall, Inc.

Murphy, M. (1959). *The Social Group Work Method in Social Work Education.* New York: Council on Social Work Education.

Ohlin, L.E. and Lawrence, W.C. (1959). "Social interaction among clients as a treatment problem", *Social Work*, 4(2), 3-13.

Pathak, S.H. (1961). *Medical social work in India* (pp. 17-25). Delhi: Delhi School of Social Work.

Perlman, H.H. (1957). *Social Case work: A Problem-solving Process.* Chicago: The University of Chicago Press.

Richmond, M.E. (1922). *What is Social Case Work?: An Introductory Description.* New York: Russell Sage Publications.

Sieder, V.M. (1959). "The Task of the community organization worker", Lurie, H.L. (Ed.), *The community organization method in social work education* (pp. 249-50). New York: Council on Social Work Education.

Trecker, G. (1955). *Social Group Work: Principles and Practices.* New York: Association Press.

Warde, S.M. (1987). "Social work in medical setting", *Encyclopedia of social work in India* (Vol. 3, pp. 172-78). New Delhi: Publication Division, Ministry of Information and Broadcasting, GOI.

5

Relevance of Contemporary Social Work in Hospitals

Apart from traditional methods of social work, other methods such as advocacy, awareness campaign, resource mobilization, public interest litigation, networking and strength-based practice are globally used by social workers though not being taught in social work curriculums. In the present study, a pioneering effort has been made to understand the relevance and extent to which social workers are using contemporary methods of social work in hospital settings.

Advocacy

Advocacy in social work has its origin in the 'social case work' that is based on an individual model of representing someone's interests. The term comes from the Latin word advocates, which means the function of an advocate is to give evidence by supporting verbally or making arguments for a cause. Advocacy is a well-established strategy for achieving social justice (Gehart and Lucas, 2007; Hoefer, 2006; Kiselica and Robinson, 2001; Miley, O'Melia and DuBois, 2007). The Canadian Association of Social Workers (2005) explicates the link between advocacy and social justice: Social workers advocate for fair and equitable access to public services and benefits. Social workers promote parallel consideration and safeguard under the legislation and confront injustices that affect the weak and deprived populations. Advocacy is often represented in the literature as a strategy more closely aligned with macro or policy practice

(Wolfer and Gray, 2007). However, social workers in direct practice are closely engaged in several issues of individual client lives, including financial, cultural, medical, legal and spiritual aspects that enable them to evaluate and interfere in many areas in which injustice may occur. The advocacy role appears to be a hand-in-glove fit with generalist practice (Hoefer, 2006; Kirst-Ashman and Hull, 2006; Walker, 2004).

"Advocacy involves a person(s), either an underprivileged person or a group or their representative, particularly pursuing their case with dominant others, about situations which either strike them directly or attempting to avoid alterations which will leave them struggling. Both the intent and outcome of such advocacy should be to increase the individual's sense of power; help them to feel more confident, to become more assertive and gain increased choices" (Brandon and Brandon, 1995). Advocacy can be directly associated with clinical work via a similar aim, that is, "supporting patients to achieve independence and exercise control over their own lives" (Lens and Gibelman, 2002). Modern social work practice frameworks have gone beyond individual problem-focused perspectives and deal with issues of power, culture, social and economic discrimination (Finn and Jacobson, 2003).

McLaughlin (2009), in a study, described three types of advocacies used by clinical social workers: instrumental advocacy, educational advocacy and practical advocacy. Instrumental advocacy is related to the specific actions taken by the subjects on behalf of clients. Educational advocacy involves heightening awareness of social justice issues, rights, needs and opportunities, not just for clients but also for colleagues or the public at large. Practical advocacy involves working with clients directly to access resources, such as accompanying them to appeals or even filling out documentation that is posing a barrier to access to resources.

Social work advocacy is the exclusive and mutual representation of clients or a cause in a forum aimed at systematically affecting the decision-making in an unfair or passive system (Schneider and Lester, 2001). The method of advocacy is very handy for social workers to achieve the goal of social justice and social welfare in the changing global scenario. The basic assumption behind the development of 'advocacy' as a method of social work is the potential role advocacy can play in providing justice to people at large, especially the vulnerable. Professional social workers should work at the behest of the client and keep in mind the client's consent and involvement in the process. The additional objective should be empowering the client and assertiveness training via modeling.

The findings of this study depict that 52.4 percent of the respondents are using advocacy on behalf of the patients to help them in the treatment of their illness. In almost all age groups, more than half of respondents were informed about its application in the practice. A greater percentage of male respondents and social workers with higher education are involved in the use of advocacy strategies.

Awareness Campaign

Sayers (2006) maintains that raising awareness about something whether good, bad or indifferent means promoting its apparentness and reliability within a community or society. Raising public awareness is not the same as telling the public what to do. It is explaining issues and disseminating knowledge to people so that they can make their own decisions. Awareness campaigns are often the first step to introduce the audience to new services, programmes, facilities or actions. It is aimed at building familiarity with desirable behavior, say, promoting immunization or improving public health. However, providing information and creating awareness about an issue does not automatically lead to behavioral change. Modifications in attitude and behavior are highly complex processes, which demand knowledge of human behaviors and then diligently initiating steps to produce the desired change in the behavior of the people. For this, people must be encouraged to move through successive stages to reach the point where new behaviors can be adapted and maintained. Social work professionals have been involved in this process by addressing crucial issues for several decades now. Campaigning is often less well understood and may be seen as a broadly organized effort to change practices, policies or behaviors. It relies on the capability of stakeholders to transmit the same message to a varied audience, applying multiple approaches.

An awareness campaign will typically embrace four key actions: researching the issue, activating support, informing the public and lobbying decision-makers. A well-designed and appropriately presented awareness-building campaign is possibly one of the most systematic and efficacious means of passing on information about a specific topic or matter to a huge and geographically scattered body of people: for example, the population of a country or a particular community within that country. Some of the popular objectives of awareness campaigns are to sensitize the target audience on specific issues, influence policymakers, increase support and gain public interest, to bridge the knowledge gap on specific issues and thereby provide the right message to the target audience, defy negative perceptions and reframe the conversation.

Information is 'power' and a pre-requisite of 'empowerment'. In almost all interventions, the primary task of trained social workers is to create awareness. An awareness campaign is extensively used to bring about desired positive change in the attitudes, perceptions and behavior of target groups and communities by providing information. The scope of the awareness campaign is very vast and includes issues like promoting family planning, anti-tobacco, drug de-addiction, road safety, disaster management, HIV/AIDS, cancer, leprosy, female feticide, women's health rights and so on.

Awareness campaigns have used case work methods extensively. In the HIV setting, while working with high-risk groups, the National Aids Control Programme has initiated Behavior Change Communication, which is one of the significant models of awareness campaigns. Social workers, in varied case work settings, make use of awareness campaigns. Some of the salient manifestations are: a client of drug abuse is enabled to 'change behavior' after creating awareness; a woman is made aware of family planning methods and encouraged to adopt one; a parent of newborn is informed about immunization services. In rural communities, youth groups are formed to create awareness on diverse topics like sanitation, public health and the prevention of communicable diseases like HIV/AIDS. Support groups of patients and caregivers of Alzheimer's, terminally ill cancer patients, people infected with HIV, people with disabilities, mental illness, etc. also make use of strategies and approaches of awareness campaigns (Kaushik, 2016).

Awareness campaigns and advocacy interventions serve a dual purpose and are often complementing each other. There are several benefits of combining awareness campaigns with resource mobilization. It promotes public relations and ensures credibility for the social work agency. The strengths-based method is something that truly guides and influences a social worker to practice as a professional. It is associated and practiced along with other social work methods to bring the optimum outcome to the clients. In this study, 75.9 percent of the respondents informed that they are making use of awareness campaign strategies to educate people on various health-related problems and their remedies. The proportion of respondents involved in awareness campaigns is substantial in all age groups, genders and education levels.

Resource Mobilization

Social work is a profession that helps society work better for people and helps people function fruitfully within society by using various methods to achieve these objectives. Resource mobilization is an integral part of the helping process wherein the social worker has to mobilize the much-needed resources for the betterment of the client/group/community. The genesis of resource mobilization not only dates to ancient India, where philanthropic activities were a drama or religion but also to several societies and nations across the globe. The concept of charity has its roots in the Vedic period. Even the Indian scriptures like *Rig Veda* mention charitable and pious work like digging water ponds for the community and temporary shelters and even offering free food for travelers. In fact, those who are well endowed are supposed to do more and more for the community at large, especially for the marginalized and deprived, with the aim of salvation through the service of humanity. It is the pivot on which the Indian socio-culture revolves. The welfare of the least has been the main motivation behind the philanthropic activities of people and institutions all over the world, including India. The entire voluntary sector/development agencies working for the vulnerable have taken up resource mobilization or fund raising to act as a catalyst for empowerment and self-sustainability. The efforts of the Associations of Fundraising Professionals (AFP) in the USA are well known among philanthropists. Resource mobilization involves helping the client with needed resources such as housing, clothing, food, furniture, financial support or healthcare. Resource mobilization is the acquisition of needed services, and it requires the knowledge of service networks (Hepworth, Rooney, and Larson, 2002).

Social work has been described as the profession that helps society work better for people, and helps people function fruitfully within the society. Many a time the client may not be aware of the various resources available, so the practitioners act as brokers by referring to resource systems such as public legal services, healthcare agencies, child welfare divisions, mental health centers, family counseling agencies, sources of financial assistance, etc. (Joseph, 2016). According to Hollis (1964) a social worker is a provider of resources either as an advocate, source of knowledge or as a person who has access to the resources of an agency. For example, residential and day care services, foster care services, rehabilitation services, transportation services, medical aid, financial help, etc.

The data obtained from the study suggests that 73.8 percent of the respondents are using the mechanisms of resource mobilization to help patients undergo treatment in hospitals in Delhi. Respondents above 41 years and female social workers are more involved in it.

Public Interest Litigation

According to *Black's Law Dictionary*, "Public Interest Litigation means a legal action initiated in a court of law for the enforcement of public interest or general interest in which the public or class of the community have pecuniary interest or some interest by which their lawful rights or liabilities are affected". Public interest litigation is not defined in any statute or any act. It has been explained by judges to think about the intention of the public at large. Before the 1980s, only the aggrieved party could personally knock on the doors of justice and seek remedy for one's grievance, and any other person who was not personally affected could not ask for justice as a representative for the victim or the aggrieved party. This entire scenario gradually changed when the post-emergency Supreme Court tackled the problem of access to justice by people through radical changes and alterations made in the requirements of locus standi and the party aggrieved. Any citizen of India/consumer group/social action group can go to the apex court of the country demanding legal resolution in all cases where the interests of the general population or a section of it are in jeopardy.

Further, public interest cases could be filed without an investment of heavy court fees as required in private civil litigation. By reinterpreting of the Right to Personal Liberty in Article 21 and the Right to Equality before the Law in Article 14, the court conferred the judiciary an extended power of review to safeguard the basic rights of citizens. PIL is one of the most powerful weapons the Judiciary in India has acquired in recent times in order to implement the legal obligation of the Executive and the Legislature. Its purpose is to give justice and assist in the promotion of the well-being of the people. According to Justice V.R. Krishna Iyer, the PIL is a process of achieving justice for the people, by voicing people's complaints through the legal process. The purpose of PIL is to render the common people of this country access to the courts to receive legal solutions against injustice done to them.

A social worker should be sufficiently equipped with knowledge of the available sources of relief—medical, economic, psychological and legal for those who are in trouble. They should be aware of laws of everyday matters and the process and procedure as it relates to their practice. Healthcare is one of the issues related to PIL. Social workers work with, on behalf or in the interest of people to enable them to deal with personal and social difficulties and obtain essential resources and services. PIL works as a tool for social reform, social welfare, development and change while reaching out to those who are neglected and powerless to address their own problems (Mathew, 2016).

An attempt was made in the present study to know the relevance of IPL in hospital social work practice. It is observed that only 13.8 percent of the respondents were using public interest litigation on behalf of the patients.

Networking

According to dictionary.com, networking is a support system for exchanging information and services among persons and groups with a common interest. In the *Oxford Dictionary*, "networking is a system of trying to meet and talk to other people who may be useful to you in your work". Miser defined networking as the process of evolving and stimulating relationships to grow the business, widen the sphere of influence or serve the community.

In social work, networking implies the establishment of cooperative and collaborative relationships with like-minded people and institutions for mutual development and support for rendering help to the clients. Through networking a professional can use contacts to acquire information, advice and referrals for people in need as well as for financial and technical support. In social work, networking is of utmost importance as a worker has to refer a client for other services which can be facilitated through other people who are working in other departments (Neeta Kumari and Rafat Ara, 2016).

Social work is widely recognized as a difficult profession for ordinary people. Challenging, complex and demanding, all social workers, at some time or other, need to know that there is support or discreet friendly advice close at hand. Yet finding that support, or even knowing where to access it, has not always been straightforward. That's where networking among social workers has become of growing importance in recent years. Often, informal sessions where like-minded professionals—or those new to social work in particular—can seek advice and support and discuss some of the challenges, opportunities and even the success they have experienced. It's an informal way of sharing best practices, as well as being a support network when times are tough. Networking is perhaps the most crucial part of people's careers, and everybody, particularly social workers and students should be exercising proper networking habits.

As social workers, we need to be leaders in our community and build successful relationships with various people, and it is important to connect with professionals in all sectors that can influence the social atmosphere. Networking can help build relationships between and among social workers, their clients and resource groups. Mutual relations drive the way our society functions because we are a social entity made up of social human beings. People are more prone to give jobs to people they like or do business with people they know.

Networking opens doors to a variety of resources inside and outside the profession. The method of networking enables social work professionals to identify various resources like expertise, funds, materials, etc., within the social work profession, other allied professions and in the larger society. This will increase the quality of social work assistance. The resources could be of different natures: contacts for implementing various methods of social work; material and financial resources; manpower and referral services; curriculum; research results; knowledge on various types of clients including indigenous people as well as best practices traditionally existing in various communities.

Networking is a matter of creating useful linkages, both within and among people, groups, communities, organizations, and societies, in order to mobilize resources as well as to support the profession in different ways. This will help in enabling social work intervention with the clients—individuals, groups, families and communities to provide various types of assistance in their best interest for maximizing results. The method of networking facilitates the effective referral of clients to appropriate professionals and agencies and ensures effective social work intervention.

In the present study, more than 70 percent of respondents informed that they are using networking skills to meet the needs of patients coming to the hospitals. A greater percent of young respondents (31%), female respondents (46.9%) and postgraduate social workers (42.1%) are making use of networking.

Strength-Based Practice

The strengths approach tries to understand clients in terms of their potential rather than the problems. This approach systematically examines the client's survival skills, abilities, knowledge, resources and desires and can be used in some way to help meet client goals (Saleebey, 1996). A strength-based approach operates on the assumption that people have strengths and resources for their own empowerment (Pulla, 2012). Empirical research suggests that strength-based interventions have a positive psychological impact, particularly in embracing individual well-being through the development of hope (Kurien, 2016).

Siegal and colleagues studied 632 subjects with substance abuse problems and ascertained that rendering strengths-based case management was related to retention in aftercare treatment. Additionally, in a follow-up study, a relationship between case management, improved retention and severity of drug use was found in the same group, as well as improved employability outcomes (Rapp et al., 1998). Kumari and Gajendragad (2015), in a case report, mentioned how a rape survivor with mental illness was assisted to cope with critical factors through the use of her innate strengths and opportunities.

Strengths-based practice is a synergic process between the person assisted by services and those assisting them, permitting them to work together to decide an outcome that relies on the person's strengths and assets. It permits one to see opportunities, hope and solutions rather than just problems and hopelessness. A real strengths-based perspective governs the way we think about people and the way we perform our work on a day-to-day basis for all actions and interactions.

It is important to understand that the strengths-based approach is not about denying that people do experience problems and challenges, and these issues do need to be taken into consideration in a more holistic approach. Strengths-based practice is a social work practice theory that lays stress on people's self-determination and strengths. It is a philosophy and a way of perceiving clients as resourceful and strong in the face of difficulty. It is client-led, with an emphasis on future possibilities and strengths that people bring to a problem or crisis. When applied beyond the field of social work, strengths-based practice is also referred to as the "strengths-based approach".

It is observed that 49.7 percent of hospital social workers in Delhi are involved in strength-based practice with the patients. More female social workers and MSW respondents are using this approach in practice.

Relevance of Contemporary Social Work Methods

In the study, the researcher attempted to know from respondents about the relevance of contemporary methods of social work in hospital social work practice. Their response was categorized into four ranges: 1. Greatly, 2. Somewhat, 3. Hardly, and 4. Not at all. It is observed that 30.3 percent of participants said that advocacy is very much relevant to hospital social work; 40 percent of respondents find it somewhat relevant; and 10.3 percent does not consider it relevant at all. Around 53.8 percent of social workers think awareness campaigns are greatly relevant and 36.6 percent think it is somewhat relevant. Resource mobilization is considered extremely important by 52.4 percent of respondents. Among all, 33.8 percent of respondents informed that PIL is hardly relevant and 15.9 percent of respondents said that it is not relevant to hospital social work practice. Half of the respondents think the great relevance of networking in their practice. About 26.9 percent of respondents were informed about the greater relevance of strength-based practice in hospital social work.

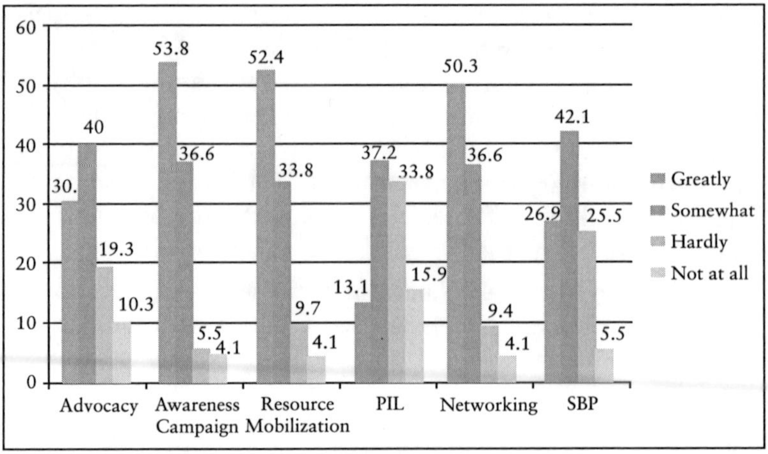

Graph 5.1: Relevance of Contemporary Social Work Methods

It is concluded that more than half of respondents are making use of advocacy in their practice; more than three-fourth of the respondents are using awareness campaign strategies; nearly three-fourth of hospital social workers are engaged in mobilizing financial, material and human resources and networking; and almost half of the respondents are involved in strength-based practice. Public interest litigation is the least practiced strategy and only a negligible number of social workers make use of PIL. As far as the relevance of contemporary methods of social work is concerned, it is found that awareness campaigns, resource mobilization and networking drew greater attention of hospital social workers, followed by advocacy and strength-based practice. The relevance of public interest litigation is found to be minimum as compared to other contemporary methods of social work.

References

Brandon, D. (1995). *Advocacy: Power to people with disabilities.* Birmingham: BASW, Venture Press.

Canadian Association of Social Workers (2005). *Code of Ethics*. Retrieved from http://www.casw-acts.ca/

Finn, J., and Jacobson, L.M. (2003). "Just practice: Steps toward a new practice paradigm." *Journal of Social Work Education*, 39(1), 57-78.

Gajendragad, J.M., and Kumari, S. (2015). "Strengths based approach in psychiatric social work—A case report", *IOSR Journal of Humanities and Social Science,* 20(4), 01-04.

Gehart, D., and Lucas, B. (2007). "Client advocacy in marriage and family therapy: A qualitative case study", *Journal of Family Psychotherapy,* 18(1), 39-56.

Hepworth, D.H., Larsen J., and Rooney, R.H. (2002). *Direct Social Work Practice: Theory and Skills.* Pacific Grove, CA: Brooks/Cole, Thomson Learning.

Hoefer, R. (2006). *Advocacy practice for social justice.* Chicago: Lyceum Books.

Hollis, F. (1964). *Case work: A psychosocial therapy.* New York: Random House.

Joseph, S. (2016). "Resource Mobilisation", Thomas, G. (Ed.), *Contemporary Methods of Social Work.* New Delhi: Shipra Publications.

Kaushik, A. (2016). "Awareness Campaign", Thomas, G. (Ed.). *Contemporary Methods of Social Work.* New Delhi: Shipra Publications.

Kirst-Ashman, K., and Hull, G. (2006). *Understanding generalist practice* (4th ed.). CA: Brooks/Cole Publishers.

Kiselica, M.S., and Robinson, M. (2001). "Bringing advocacy counseling to life: The history, issues, and human dramas of social justice work in counseling", *Journal of Counseling & Development,* 79(4), 387-97.

Kumari, N., and Ara, R. (2016). "Networking", G. Thomas (Ed.). *Contemporary Methods of Social Work.* New Delhi: Shipra Publications.

Kurian, A. (2016). "Strength Based Practice Method", G. Thomas (Ed.), *Contemporary Methods of Social Work.* New Delhi: Shipra Publications.

Lens, V., and Gibelman, M. (2000). "Advocacy, be not forsaken: Retrospective lessons from welfare reform", *Families in Society,* 18(6), 611-20.

Mathew, P.D. (2016). "Public Interest Litigation", G. Thomas (Ed.). *Contemporary Methods of Social Work.* New Delhi: Shipra Publications.

McLaughlin, A.M. (2009). "Clinical social workers: Advocates for social justice", *Advances in Social Work,* 10(1), 51-68.

Miley, K.K., O'Melia, M., and DuBois, B. (2007). *Generalist Social Work Practice: An Empowerment Approach* (5th ed.). Boston: Allyn & Bacon.

Pulla, V. (2012). “What is strength practice all about?”, Pulla, V., Chenoweth, L., Francis, A., Bakaj, S. (Eds.), *Papers in Strength Based Practice*. New Delhi: Allied Publications.

Rapp et al. (1998). Predicting post-primary treatment services and drug use outcome: A multivariate analysis. *American Journal of Drug and Alcohol Abuse*, 24(4), 603-15.

Richard, S. (2006). *Principles of awareness raising for information literacy: A case study*. Thailand: Communication Information, UNESCO.

Saleebey, D. (1996). “The strengths perspective in social work practice: Extensions and cautions”, *Social Work*, 41, 296-305.

Schneider, R.L., and Lester, L. (2001), *Social Work Advocacy: A New Framework for Action*. Belmont, CA: Wadsworth/Thomson Learning.

Thomas, G. (Ed.). (2015). *Contemporary Methods of Social Work*. Delhi: Shipra Publication.

Walker, S. (2004). “Community work and psychosocial practice: Chalk and cheese or birds of a feather?”, *Journal of Social Work Practice*, 18(2), 161-75.

Wolfer, T., and Gray, K. (2007). “Using the decision case method to teach policy advocacy”, *Journal of Teaching in Social Work*, 27(1-2), 37-59.

6

Major Findings, Conclusions and Suggestions

This chapter puts forward major findings and conclusions related to demographic characteristics and tasks of hospital social workers; application and relevance of conventional and contemporary social work in hospitals; and status and extent of job satisfaction of professional social workers in hospital settings in Delhi, which have been drawn on the basis of the primary data. Concrete suggestions have also been given to further consolidate medical social work practice in hospital settings.

Personal Profile

It was observed that among the 145 respondents, the majority of hospital social workers (68.3%) in Delhi were young, falling into the 20-40 age range. A higher percentage (75.2%) of respondents in the study belonged to the general category. Just (9%) of respondents worked for private hospitals, compared to (65.5%) of respondents who were employed by central government hospitals. This indicated that despite the guidelines in place, the state government and private hospitals were not very keen to appoint medical social workers. The majority of the social workers (62.8%) in the study had experience in the range of ten years. This data helped to conclude that there were more number of job openings in the last ten years for MSW candidates in the hospitals in Delhi. Slightly over half of hospital social workers (51%) were working in permanent positions.

Overall 29 percent of respondents with five years of experience were contractual, which means that a greater number of young respondents were working on a contractual basis. There was a disparity in the salary structure between regular and contractual hospital social workers in Delhi.

Educational Profile

The basic qualification of the majority of respondents (85.5%) was Post Graduation in Social Work. Undergraduate and Diploma programs in social work commenced much later and are offered by only a few institutions. Therefore, the number of respondents having a BSW degree or diploma was less as compared to other degrees.

Nomenclature of the Post Graduate Degree

The nomenclature of the post graduate degree obtained by the hospital social workers in the majority of cases (62.1%) was MSW (Masters in Social Work) and (23.4%) M.A. (Social Work).

Specialization in Degree Course

The Bhore Committee emphasized specialized training in hospital social work following which courses in medical and psychiatric social work were commenced by social work teaching institutions. However, in the current study, it was observed that only 20.7 percent of the respondents held specialization in medical and psychiatric social work. Hence, the findings of the study imply that hospitals were not much concerned about specialization or background training while recruiting social workers in hospital settings in Delhi.

Research Qualifications

As regards research qualifications, it was found that only a minimal percent of respondents (6.9%) did M.Phil. and (3.4%) held Ph.D. in Social Work/Psychiatric Social Work qualifications. This further stipulates that hospital social workers were not very keen on upgrading their qualifications despite working for many years in the field of medical social work.

Functions of Hospital Social Workers

The study revealed that social workers in hospital settings were involved in multiple activities related to direct patient services (counseling psychosocial study, home visits, referral and resource mobilization), administration, teaching, training, supervision and research.

Problems Addressed by Hospital Social Workers

The findings of the study revealed that the economic or financial issues of the patients, particularly, poor and indigent patients; housing or accommodation-related issues of the outstation patients and their relocation; helping patients in navigating hospital systems and procedures; dealing with the beliefs and value system of the patients; inadequate community resources; personality problems and communication problems were the major issues addressed by hospital social workers.

Application of Traditional Social Work Methods

In this study, an attempt was made to describe the application of conventional social work methods by social workers in exercising their duties in hospitals. The majority of respondents informed that they are making use of social case work techniques in their practice. Slightly more than half of the social workers were applying the methods of social group work, social research and social welfare administration whereas community organization and social action were the least used methods for social workers in hospital settings.

Relevance of Contemporary Methods of Social Work

It is concluded that awareness campaigns, resource mobilization and networking drew greater attention of hospital social workers followed by advocacy and strength-based practice. The relevance of public interest litigation is found minimal as compared to other contemporary methods of social work.

Workplace Environment

It is observed in the study more than half of the respondents did not have independent rooms or cabins and they were sharing rooms with other staff of the hospital. In all, 74.5 percent of respondents were provided with a telephone facility; 75.9 percent of hospital social workers had a computer facility available to them; 56.6 percent of respondents were provided with hospital attendants and 53.8 percent of respondents were working without any transport facility or allowance. About 84 percent of respondents were working in Day Shift; 9.7 percent of the respondents were working in two shifts (Morning and Evening Shift); 6.2 percent of the respondents were working in three shifts and 17.9 percent of the respondents informed that they remained on call and may be called upon to come to the hospital whenever required. While 35.9 percent of the respondents reported a very heavy workload; 51 percent of the respondents informed that their workload was somewhat heavy. About 31.7 percent of the respondents reported that they formally place their complaints; 24.8 percent of the respondents were doing it in informal ways; 42.8 of the respondents informed that they used to place their grievances in a both formal and informal manner and 0.7 percent of the respondents stated that they do not place their grievances.

Professional Development

About 88 percent of respondents informed that there was no refresher course or continuing education in which they could participate from time to time. Only a few respondents informed that they quite often participated in seminars, conferences or workshops pertaining to social work. The majority of the respondents had not participated in organizing any academic activity in their department. Among all, 54.5 percent of the respondents informed that there was no social work literature available in the hospital library. Nearly 40 percent of respondents informed that their duties were not defined by the hospital management at the time of joining, so they were not clear about the duties to be performed and the expectations by the authorities. The majority of respondents informed that there were no opportunities for promotion to higher grades in the current job. The data obtained from the study depicts that the work of the majority of hospital social workers (65.5%)

was supervised by medical professionals. Only 23.4 percent of respondents were supervised by senior social workers. Hence, it is concluded that the authority who supervises the work of social workers belongs to a Non-Social Science background like medical personnel or administrators who may not be aware of the roles and functions of hospital social work practice. Nearly 61 percent of respondents informed that there was no association of social workers in hospitals. Among all, 41.4 percent of the respondents informed that teamwork is greatly encouraged at their workplace.

Extent of Job Satisfaction

Only 13.1 percent of the respondents stated that they were fully satisfied with the salary, 51 percent of the respondents were satisfied to some extent and 35.9 percent of the respondents were not satisfied at all with the salary. As regards work facilities, only 8.6 percent of respondents were fully satisfied with work facilities being provided to them and 60.7 percent of respondents were satisfied to some extent. Nearly 17 percent of the respondents appeared fully satisfied with opportunities for training and continuing education given to the hospital's social workers, 35.9 percent were satisfied to some extent and 47.6 percent of the respondents were not satisfied with the training efforts and opportunities in their hospitals. As far as the relationship with other colleagues at the workplace is concerned, 52.4 percent of the respondents were fully satisfied. With healthcare teams, 40.7 percent of the respondents are fully satisfied and 50.3 percent of the respondents are somewhat satisfied. As regards responding to the needs of patients and their families, 55.2 percent of the respondents are fully satisfied and 42.1 percent of the respondents are somewhat satisfied. In overall job satisfaction, 26.2 percent of the respondents in the study expressed their full satisfaction in their current job, 60 percent of the respondents were satisfied to some extent only and the remaining 13.8 percent of respondents said that they were not satisfied with their present job. Overall satisfaction is lower when analyzed according to gender, experience and type of hospital. More male respondents in the early years of their jobs and working in state and private hospitals are dissatisfied with their jobs.

Findings of the study that are of professional concerns:

1. Limited application of conventional social work methods except social case work by medical social workers.
2. Insufficient engagement in professional guidance and supervision as well as in teaching and training of different professions.
3. Minimal participation in conferences, seminars, symposiums, etc.
4. Decline in home visits as a tool of social work.
5. Lack of training in medical social work generates the necessity for in-service training for medical social workers to bring change in their knowledge, skills and attitude.
6. Limited participation of hospital social workers in budget preparation, policy and programme formulation and representation in hospital committees.
7. Absence of supervision of medical social workers by professionally qualified persons.
8. Non-availability of professional social work literature in hospital libraries.
9. Low level of job satisfaction due to low salary, fewer opportunities for promotions, poor work facilities, etc.
10. Indifference of the medical social workers towards forming associations with fellow professionals.
11. Absence of purposeful interaction among hospital social workers.
12. Reluctance among hospital social workers to upgrade their qualifications.
13. Absence of an appropriate policy for the appointment of hospital social workers.

An important conclusion that may be derived from this study is that the image of hospital social workers needs to be improved. The responsibility for improving the image lies with professional social workers, hospitals, schools of social work, professional organization and the government.

Suggestions

Based on the findings, the following recommendations pertaining to the responsibilities of hospital social workers, hospital authorities, social work institutions, professional organizations and government have been laid down.

Responsibilities of Hospital Social Workers

The professionally trained social workers have the responsibility to use their professional knowledge and skills for the benefit of clients. They work in settings where they can easily locate various target groups such as children, adolescent boys and girls, women, older people and people suffering from ill health or disability. Meaningful use of social work methods is called for. The role of hospital-based social workers has many dimensions such as that of advocate, mediator, enabler, teacher, therapist and resource provider. By and large, the social workers have been playing the role of resource mobilizer. They need to play the other different dimensions of his/her role. It should be a matter of professional concern and interest that they seize all the opportunity to project their role, making it visible to patients, doctors, nurses and administrators. In social work, the self-awareness of the worker is conventionally thought of as part of the development of the professional self, which is taught in relation to the teaching skill. Self-awareness is discussed here as knowledge because it begins with the recognition that the social worker's own attitudes are vital in influencing performance and understanding how these responses operate. Everyone has to learn this through his own feelings and doing, not intellectually. But for the person, it is part of the body of professional knowledge. Moreover, in each field of social work practice, there are situations and characteristics of that field, which present crucial problems to the social worker in terms of his/her own attitudes and responses. Successful performance in the field depends upon the ability to deal with one's own attitude in relation to these recurrent situations.

A second group of emotion-evoking situations has to do with the conditions under which work is executed in a hospital setting. Social workers should accept the discipline of sharing the patient with medicine and other professions. This implies readiness to take up the appropriate social work role in the medical team, with acceptance of medical authority and acknowledgement of the middle-level status of social work. It also means acceptance of the tempo and inevitable interruptions of medical care without too much frustration. These are factors that operate less harshly than those related to mutilation and death, but they are still disturbing to most social workers and must be faced. Hospital social worker also needs to develop a link with the professional organizations of social work and other organizations working in the area of health-related issues. The future growth and development of the field of medical social work, largely depend upon the efforts made by medical social workers, in successfully handling these problems.

Responsibilities of Hospitals

Hospital settings are all operating on a medical science approach exclusive of social science orientations. The outcome of adopting this approach is that the deficiencies and contractions of the social structures and social and emotional factors affecting the patient which are detrimental to the patient's conditions of ill health are often overlooked by the administrators. In large complex hospital settings, the social work profession is represented by one or two professionals employed in the settings. Hospital social worker needs to have adequate physical facilities and support of clerical assistance so that they can be more efficient in their role performance and the time can be utilized for performing legitimate professional tasks. Medical Settings are bureaucratic organizations. It is crucial that the settings provide ample opportunities for promotion and adequate scales to the social workers. It is also vital that administrators are clear about the role of social workers. The administrators who are clear about the role of the hospital social workers will have higher expectations from them. The setting should have an administrative mechanism for providing regular supervision for medical social workers and for demanding accountability from them. Hospitals employing social workers must encourage them to update their knowledge from time to time and provide sufficient opportunities for learning and keeping in touch with new professional developments in the field. The settings must develop the 'Team Concept' and create a mechanism in the settings by which it can be practiced.

Responsibilities of Schools of Social Work

It is necessary to examine whether social work graduates are able to use the knowledge and skills acquired during their training. If the graduates are not using the acquired knowledge and skills in these areas of professional practice, as this study points out, it should be a matter of concern for the schools of social work. The schools of social work must investigate and ascertain the reasons which may be associated with one or more of the following factors:

- Irrelevance of curriculum for the job content of social workers.
- Inappropriate attitude and characteristics of social work graduates.
- Shortcomings and deficiencies of the employing organizations regarding the responsibility of utilizing the service of social workers effectively.
- Inadequacy of fieldwork training during the course. Schools of social work also have to find remedies for the above problems.

Responsibilities of Professional Organizations of Social Work

All the professionals are organized into some kind of professional association. These professional associations serve three purposes:

- To provide ways and means of improving the professional performance of the individuals.
- To exercise appropriate social control of the professionals in order to ensure competent performance by the individuals.

- To protect the member's exclusive right to practice their profession.

Professional social workers should realize their responsibility to form such an organization. The organization thus formed has to be dynamic and raise issues relevant to the profession for the benefit of the clients whom they serve. Professional organizations have the responsibility to provide opportunities for continuing education so that the professionals can keep their knowledge up to date. One of the major responsibilities of the professional organization is to study the relevant changes taking place at the political level and policy level and its implications for medical social work and the target groups, whom the professionals serve. The organization also should make efforts to bring about necessary changes.

Government Responsibility

The committee appointed by the Government of India in 1946 was responsible for creating a new professional group of hospital-based social workers for the first time in the country. The committee described the role of medical social worker and their functions six decades ago. Since then, the healthcare sector has undergone numerous alterations at the structural and functional levels, thereby bringing about changes also in social work responsibilities and tasks. Hence, there is a need now to review these functions in the changing contexts of the twenty-first century. A definite policy for the appointment of hospital social workers is required to be established and maintained. It is the task of the government to frame an appropriate policy indicating the specialized qualifications required for the hospital social worker and delineating the job content.

Social work professionals working in healthcare settings cannot be effective without various systems like provisions for economic assistance to poor patients and the creation of various support services for the rehabilitation of patients. Since India is a welfare state, it is the responsibility of the government to provide necessary support systems to facilitate treatment services in the medical settings. In brief, one may say that hospital social worker has to change their ways of functioning and there have to be changes in the official and professional networks so that the sick and disabled requiring social services may have a better deal.

This study indicated that like the teaching profession, more female social workers are working in hospital settings. The majority of the respondents belong to the general category. Central government hospitals have appointed more social workers as compared to state government-run hospitals. In private hospitals, the number of social workers is negligible. A large number of respondents are contractual employees. There exist disparities in the salary and promotional avenues for hospital social workers though the essential qualifications of recruitment are the same for the majority of the respondents. Hospital authorities are not very keen on the specialization of candidates when recruiting them. Respondents are not interested in upgrading their qualifications. Respondents have spent most of their time providing direct patient services like counseling, referrals, resource mobilization, meeting medical teams, admission and home visits. Few of them are engaged in administrative work, data collection, teaching, training and supervision. Economic problems, hospital procedures and lack of community resources are the major problems encountered by respondents.

Some of the findings of the study are concerned with the social work profession. Except for case work techniques, hospital social workers are not able to make adequate use of other conventional methods of social work. On the other hand, respondents reported substantial relevance of contemporary methods of social work (advocacy, awareness campaign, resource mobilization, PIL, networking and strength-based practice) in hospital social work practice. Hospital authorities do not consult social workers in budget formulation, programme and policy-making and representation in hospital committees. The majority of hospital social workers are not supervised by their senior social workers. Only a small number of respondents have participated in or organized seminars, conferences and other academic activities. There is a low level of job satisfaction due to low salaries, fewer opportunities for promotions and inadequate work facilities.

Hospital social work is an important area of social work practice. There is a need to develop this field which requires concentrated efforts by trained social workers, hospitals, schools of social work, professional associations and the government. Professional social workers employed in medical settings should take every opportunity to project their role among medical experts and hospital administration. Hospital authorities should also provide adequate facilities and opportunities for their professional growth. Social work training institutions should examine and revise the contents of the curriculums and fieldwork training and remove deficiencies so that hospital social workers are able to make effective use of social work methods while discharging their duties. A professional organization should play a dynamic role to raise the issues relevant to hospital social workers and facilitate their continuing education. An appropriate policy for the appointment of professional social workers in hospital settings needs to be formulated and implemented by the government.

Index